THE
ROADMAP

Navigating Your Way to Leadership Success

Cameron Morrissey

ISBN-10: 1539502236
ISBN-13: 978-1539502234

For My Parents & Grandparents

Who showed me the roadmap to success in life

TABLE OF CONTENTS

ACKNOWLEDGEMENTS

No endeavor succeeds without the help of many people. For me, that help came through The Roadmap Feedback Team. A group of people who didn't mind suffering through all of my spelling and grammatical errors, and who were kind enough to give me honest feedback on what worked in "The Roadmap" and what didn't. This book wouldn't be nearly what it is today without each and every one of you. From the bottom of my heart, I thank:

Agusta Long, Alan Blue, Allan Draper, Andrew Jena, Angela Bouler, Angie Mcfarland, Ashley Brown, Bill Wesolowski, Bob Hutchins, Charlie Keith, Jason Hensley, Jerry Williams, Sheldon Watkins, Bobbie Wilcoxen, Bonny Scott-Sleight, Brad Garpetti, Brandie Ridley, Brian Dalmas, Brigitte De La Rive, Casey Woods, Cathryn Epstein, Cathy Burnstei, Charissa Yavtucovich HR Specialist/Executive Pastor, Cherie McCann, Chris Aldridge, Chriss Waidell, Christina Blackwell, Cierra Britton, Clarence Richer, Consuela Smith, Corri L. Wilson, Damon Krick - Saren Restaurants, Danyale Davis, David M. Dangler, Dawn Deyo, BSN, RN, Dawn Sweet, Dawn Zuger, Dina Allen, Dina Rager, Donna Bucek, Elesha M. Pledger MBA, Elicia Torres, Erica E. Calhoun, Evangelea Morgan, Felecia Liggins, Fernando Mendoza, Frank Sousa, Gracie L. Snyder, Gregory Podsiadlo Sr., Hayley Skargon, Heather Welch, Heidi Brau, Heidi Nuzzo, Hendrien Hodson, Isaac Williams, Jaclyn Rohrman, Jaime Exler, Jamison Felton, Janet Melancon, Janice Lam Snyder, Jasmine Allen, Jason Hollenbach, Jason Hunt, Jeffrey M. Shaw M.Ed., Jennifer Lynn, Jennifer Weisgal, Jenny Sippel-Tompkins, Jessica J. Stoddard, Jodi Carrigan, Joe Thornton, Jonathan Leinberger, Judy Edwards, Julie Wiltse, Karla A. Nichols, Kathy J, Katrina Copson, Kay Degiobbi, Kelli Johnson, Kelly Brown, Korrie Sprong, Laurie, Lea Ovens, Lee Weissmuller, Lerato Nkosi, Lewis Mandel, Linda Bhatty, Lisa Kortum, Martin 'virtualnerd' Lindsay, Marty Johnson, Mary Jane Polbo, Matt

Rabe, Melanie Christians, Melanie Juan, Melendi Morton, Melinda Clift, Melissa Goins, Michael Morris, Michael Murphy, Michelle Bierman, Michelle L. Washington, Mishell Perez, Mohammad Mehdi Dadgostar, Mpho Mahlaba, Mrs Emma Fletcher, Nancy Arroyo, Natasha Harding, Nathan Atkinson, Nikki Washington, Nora Haase, Pam Saffell, Pamela Van Why, Patricia Robertson, Paula Gough, Phil Gould, Rachael Tyler, Raquel Johnson, Rayann Gillon, Raymon Marin, Rebecca Cassidy, Richard G. Brody, Rick Langley, Ricky Campbell, Robert P. Holcomb, Roberta Thacker-Oliver, Ronda Wolf, Rui Barcelos, Sandi Cooper, Sandra Stewart DeVault, Sandy Kocher, Sarah Abdel-Hadi, Shannon Vinter, Shawn T. Lewis, Sheila Leeper, Shelby Gagnon, Sherry Mincic, Simeon So, Stacey (Vaughan) Scott, Stacie Lamkin, Stephanie Robinson Greathouse, Steve Bragg, Susan McCloud, Susie Kientz, Takwa Hamed, Tamara Smock, Tanya Hazelwood, Tara Foley, Tess Chura, Theresa Portillo, Thomas Pizano Jr., Tiffany W, Tom Halpenny, Vibha Sabhlok, Yvonne Smith

PREFACE

There is an epidemic of poor leadership in organizations today. The reason is simple; few people get any sort of effective leadership training. Leaders today aren't allowed the opportunity to hone their skills, or even learn new ones. Whether the reason is tightening budgets or just a lack of interest, it seems that training managers to be leaders has just moved to the "back burner" for most organizations. I use the term epidemic because it spreads. Poor leaders set poor examples for those who will follow in their footsteps, and tend not to hire great leaders underneath them. Given this vacuum, it's no wonder that great leadership is so rare. My intent with this book is to fill that leadership training gap by covering some of the main issues many leaders face. There will be many leadership tactics and practices that:

- You have never heard of before
- You needed to be reminded of
- Represent the next logical step in what you already do

I have tried to make the tactics discussed as practical and approachable as possible, and I'm confident that any leader can get something out of each critical area. It was a great experience putting this together and I'm so happy to be able to get this in the hands of leaders around the world.

Enjoy!

Cameron Morrissey

INTRODUCTION

This book sets out to give some clarity to why you struggle in 10 critical areas of leadership, and seeks to give you a roadmap to become better, and eventually great. These areas of leadership were chosen based on their importance and prevalence to you at any stage of your career. They are the foundation for addressing more complicated and specific concerns as you come across them. To assist in the journey to great leadership each chapter will contain the following structure:

"Dead End" Questions – Situational questions designed to see if the results you are getting from your leadership are indicative of a problem in a particular area.

Chapter Intro – Introducing the topic, and the positives and negatives surrounding it.

"Wrong Turn" Issues – Why it is that leaders make mistakes surrounding the area of leadership, and the excuses they tell themselves.

How to Be Better – Practical methods and tactics for improving, most of which you can implement immediately in your organization.

A Pothole to Avoid – One of the primary mistakes you may be tempted to make as you seek to address an area of leadership.

How to Be Great – Some deeper methods and tactics for improving towards mastery. Again, most can be implemented immediately in your organization.

Road Work Ahead – Turning the learning into action in ways that can provide you with quick results.

"Expressway" suggestions – Simple techniques that can be employed for the leader under a time crunch.

"Start Driving" actions – One topic you plan to take action on in the coming days and weeks. Questions within this area will focus you on action and accountability.

Souvenirs From The Trip – Overview of the topics discussed and what new knowledge or tactic you will be able to use in your leadership.

The key to getting the most out of this book is action. Take the Road Work Ahead exercises, fill out the Start Driving questions, and above all, look for ways to apply these tactics immediately in your operation. There is something in every chapter that can improve your leadership and bolster your organization. Don't just find it, use it.

If you find yourself not relating to one of the chapters, that's fine, just be aware that you may see it at some other point in your career. This book is meant to be a resource that can be revisited as one's career progresses and where a new environment may present new challenges. The ideas, principles and tactics are timeless. So focus on what speaks to you in this first reading, then after you've applied your learning and have grown, come back to it. Leadership is a journey and we are constantly learning along the way.

1 Listening

Without information you can't lead effectively

2 Prioritizing

3 Delegation

4 Communication

5 Micromanagement

6 Dealing with Failure

7 Hiring

8 Team Building

9 Motivation

10 Developing Yourself

Listening

Without information you can't
lead effectively

WHEN YOU LISTEN, **YOU LEARN.** WHEN YOU LEARN, **YOU MAKE BETTER DECISIONS.** WHEN YOU MAKE BETTER DECISIONS, **YOU BECOME A BETTER LEADER.**

Are You Heading Down a Dead End?

When talking to people are you scanning the room or looking at your smartphone?

How many times has something gone wrong, and you look back and see the warning signs were there all along?

Do you find yourself asking people to repeat key parts of a conversation?

Do you interrupt people while they are talking and interject your thoughts?

Is nobody listening to you?

Great Leaders Listen Better

You can't lead if you don't have enough information to understand the situation at hand. That is why listening is so critical to great leadership. It is one of the foundational sources of information. Sure, you have a bunch of reports and metrics, but those can only take you so far. Reports don't help you brainstorm ideas as well as your team, metrics can't identify all of the things that are going right and wrong, and here's one more thing; they both lie. Ask anyone who has created a report and they will tell you there are all kinds of "artistic licenses" that can be taken in what is included and how it is presented. Reports and metrics also have underlying logic to them that often doesn't account for everything that is intended.

Listening to your team gives you access to more eyes, ears, and brains. It allows you to see and hear everything that is going on in the operation and the customer interaction. Not only do you get more and better information, but it's also an insurance policy against missing things. What few leaders understand is that they don't know what they don't know. Humans have blind spots, reports don't uncover certain issues, and leaders can't observe every single issue and transaction.

When teams listen well to each other, they all upgrade the information they have to make all of their decisions. As the old saying goes, "None of us is as smart as all of us."

Why Leaders Take a Wrong Turn

Overestimating their own knowledge

Many leaders have an inflated ego and discount the specific knowledge of team employees because they don't have as much knowledge about "all" of the organization's pieces. They don't listen for what they can learn, they reinforce what they already knew. They don't acknowledge the importance of the issue to the individual employee, they think about how small it is in the grand scheme of things.

Many leaders are afraid to not know something. So when new information is presented, they quickly look for faulty logic, assumptions, or small details that are wrong in order to dismiss it. This is the primary reason egotistical leaders stunt their career growth; they aren't taking in and processing information the right way. Basically, they aren't listening.

Too busy

Leaders don't listen because they don't have time, there's always something else to do, and always somewhere else to be. But they really don't have time not to listen. If they don't know what's important and where opportunities reside, they're wasting their time, as well as the organization's. Listening doesn't cost leaders time, it saves leaders time.

Too focused on action

"I don't have time to listen to my team, I have things to do." Or the other refrain, "Most of the time, what they say isn't important anyway." What leaders produce and get out of their decisions relies entirely on the information they have available to them to make decisions. Listening consistently to their team, their customers, their peers, and their boss ensures they have all of the relevant information to make the best decision. If leaders aren't listening to their employees, they risk just guessing.

How to Be Better

It's not you, it's me

Your listening skills are primarily stunted by your focus on yourself and your needs instead of the other person and their needs. That's at the heart of why everyone gets distracted, thinks about "more important things," and tries to rush away to something else. They are focused on themselves, not the other person.

You can't truly understand what the other person is trying to tell you, unless you focus on why they are telling it to you and what they are getting out of letting you know. Have you ever brought up a recurring issue with your boss and had them hurriedly fix the current case, but not address how to stop it from happening again? That's an example of the wrong focus. When you listen, there is a natural tendency to want to:

- Fix
- Control
- Confirm your point of view
- Gain approval
- Avoid conflict
- Be right

Being aware of these tendencies is the first step in fixing them, but to get to the heart of so many of the above issues, there is one question you can ask when listening to someone that makes the conversation squarely about them:

"If you were me, what would you do?"

Nine times out of ten, the employee bringing you feedback knows exactly what they want you to do. This takes all of the "me, me, me" out of the conversation for you and clearly helps you understand what they want to get out of the conversation with you.

Conversational ping-pong

Find yourself cutting people off? Are you being told you don't have the whole story? You might be focusing too much on listening to respond, instead of listening to understand. This is one of the most common ways to try to deal with being too busy. You want people to "cut to the chase", "get to the point", or you think you know where they are going with the discussion, so you already know what you are going to do.

Stop thinking about what you are going to say, and start thinking about what is being said. A few ideas that will help you get there:

Wait till they are done – Seems so simple, but if you know you're going to wait until they finish, you will naturally pay more attention to what is being said instead of looking for an opening to interject. Often we are talking about 30-60 seconds that you need to wait, but even when it's longer, that just means you'll learn more. Good listeners never hear people say the phrase "let me finish my thought."

Defer judgement – How often is the comment you fought so hard to interject into the conversation rendered a waste of time because you hadn't heard some very important details yet? Skip the judgement until you've heard the whole case.

Repeat what they said – Most people say that this is where you check whether you understood what they said, and that's true. But it also gives you a chance to coach them on how you'd like to hear things, and provides a natural segue into what you think about things.

Listening without interruption not only allows you to get the whole story and understand things better, it also allows the employee to practice thinking and speaking, shows them respect, and encourages them to listen to what you have to say without interruption.

EXPRESSWAY

Go on Walkabout – If you want to listen to something, you need to be within range of hearing about it. If you want to be able to see how the operation really functions, you need to get out of your office and physically see it. It is then you will be able to gather information on what is going right, wrong, what's being done as expected, and what isn't.

The other thing is it creates what is known as "collisions". Collisions are instances where you and someone else have an unexpected interaction which breaks up the routine and creates opportunities for discussion. Remember the time someone said, "Hey, since you're here_____"? Many times you would have never heard whatever is housed in that blank spot if you weren't just walking by.

"Nature gave us one tongue and two ears **so we could hear twice as much as we speak."**

~Epictetus

Let's get physical

It takes effort to listen, and too many leaders consider listening to be a passive endeavor (just look around at the next big meeting you attend). The concept of active listening helps you physically combat this passivity and better engage with the person speaking.

Eye contact – If you want to be more attentive, then you need to pay attention. That means eliminating all of the distractions in the surrounding world. Looking somebody in the eye when they speak is confirmation you aren't being distracted. I even recommend going so far as to look at the phone when you're on a conference call.

Lean in – Have you ever wanted to end a conversation so bad you started taking steps toward the door, leaning back in your chair, or looking around for an exit? Literally leaning into the conversation is the opposite of that. If you physically lean in to the person speaking or scoot forward in your chair, it shows you are interested and engaged in what they are speaking about.

Nodding your head – This is a way of confirming for them you understood what they said. It also encourages them to continue speaking and explaining their point. And a trick for those who work on the phone is to smile even though the other person can't see you, they're likely to hear it in your voice.

Simply smiling – It's welcoming and lets them know you are pleased they brought this to your attention. By way of this, it's one of the best ways to encourage future discussions to take place.

Your body and your mind influence each other. Make sure you are using your body in the right way when someone is talking to you, and your mind will more easily follow what is being said.

Please sir, could I have some more?

Here's a hard truth for most leaders; you aren't getting the whole story. Even when people bring you questions and information, even people with whom you've built up great communication and trust, will likely leave information out for a variety of reasons:

- They don't think you're interested
- They don't want to step on toes (yours or others)
- They don't want to be wrong
- They don't want to make you look like you're uninformed
- They are uncomfortable

Great listeners know to ask the probing questions to uncover more, or simply use the catch-all, "What else can you tell me?" If you don't know when to ask for more information, then you likely aren't listening well enough in the first place.

Change the channel

When you watch TV, do you just leave it on one channel all day long? No, of course not, you look for something interesting. One of the areas where you can improve your leadership is to stop waiting for people to come to you so you can listen to them, and instead go out and look for a channel to give you the information you need:

- *Customers:* Needs, Wants, What's great, What isn't?
- *Employees:* What's Working, What Isn't, Opportunities, How you can help?
- *Peers:* Common struggles, Outside opinions.
- *Boss:* Expectations, Organizational vision, Priorities.

A well rounded leader makes sure to look at all of the channels from time to time so they are up to date on the complete picture. Remember, you don't know what you don't know, so you need to expose yourself to situations that will uncover opportunities to learn.

A Pothole to Avoid

Leaders fail when they fail to act on what they see and hear. No amount of great listening will help you as a leader if you don't take action on what you hear. Utilizing the information you've learned is the payoff for the effort you've put in to listen. Action is also the proof to those who you listen to that the time and effort they took to speak to you was worth it. If they don't see the benefit in speaking with you, eventually they won't. So before you spend all of your focus improving your listening skills, don't forget that you need to be acting as well.

How to Be Great

Get formal

One of the best ways to hold yourself accountable for listening is to make it natural and routine. Set up a structure that makes it easy to hit all of the audiences you need to ensure you are in touch with everything you need to be.

Customers – Do you have feedback forms available? Do you do random surveys? Do you have a procedure for disseminating customer feedback up the chain of command all the way from the front-line through your boss?

Employees – 360 degree reviews, AMA (ask me anything) sessions, suggestion box, one-on-one meetings, staff meetings.

Peers – Round-table weekly meetings to discuss what everyone has on their plate that week, regular lunch meetings, accountability partners (a peer who holds you accountable to what you say you are going to do).

Boss – You likely have several weekly, bi-weekly, and monthly meetings on certain areas you mutually attend, and hopefully regular one-on-one meetings as well. Each of these "standard" meetings should be an opportunity for you to listen, not only to the subject matter, but for more information dealing with expectations and vision.

The more you listen, the more knowledge you will gain. If you set up a schedule and structure for "feeding your mind" it's easier to stay on top of the knowledge you need.

Find the quiet ones

The people with the best insight, ideas, and perspective are routinely your quietest employees. Why? Because they spend their time listening instead of talking. Remember the beginning of this chapter? They have listened and learned, and for that reason are just as likely to have more knowledge than anyone. Now there are two kinds of quiet employees, the introverts and the disenchanted employees, and both can be a wealth of information.

Introverts – These can be your "eyes and ears" when you aren't around. They see things from a different perspective, and for that reason can give you insight into things you think are working, but aren't, and vice-versa. While everybody else on the team may have shared their ideas, these individuals may not have. Engage with them regularly to keep abreast of what they see and think.

Disenchanted – They are frustrated about something which makes them likely to give you the information others are afraid to give you, or they are disengaged for some reason. If the latter is the case, it's important to have the conversation to get them re-engaged and figure out what went wrong. In the case of the former, then it's information you definitely need to hear, and they might be the only ones with motivation to tell you.

So invite both types of individuals into your office one by one, or have a semi-private conversation out in the department, and ask them what things they see, what's working, and what isn't.

EXPRESSWAY

Enjoy The Silence – Have you ever been in a meeting where there is an uncomfortable silence, and after a few seconds someone finally blurts out the answer to the unanswered question or says what everyone was thinking? That's the power of silence. Silence is the best friend of great listeners. As mentioned in the example, silence lets the other party know you want to listen, you want an answer, and you aren't just interested in what you think, but what they think. So if you want to be a good listener, get used to silence. After all, it's hard to listen when you're talking at the same time.

Be Sherlock Holmes

Listening is about so much more than the words that are said. Reading the body language of the person you are listening to can let you know how they feel about the topic and give you a better idea of how you need to react. Have you ever had an employee come up to you in a hurried panic? Did you give them your full attention? Did you act quickly? This is an example of reading body language and changing how you listen. You saw "crisis" written all over their body language, pace of speech, and tone. A few of the more common emotions and what you can infer from them:

Excited – Someone who is excited about an opportunity probably wants to be a part of it, and probably wants action from you right away. They move quickly, talk quickly and are likely to hold your gaze until they get the response they are looking for.

Unsure – Someone who is unsure about something needs reassurance and it might be worthwhile to check on the information they are providing. They talk slower, don't make eye contact, and often end sentences with tonal question marks.

Confident – When someone is confident you can be more sure of the information they have given you. They maintain eye contact, have a straighter posture, and talk in an even tone. Just make sure they don't have a history of using confidence as a means of getting their way. Trust, but verify.

Taking words at face value without taking into account the non-verbal cues could leave you missing information, taking the wrong action, or making the wrong decision.

"The people with the best insight, ideas, and perspective are routinely **your quietest employees.** Why? Because they spend their time **listening instead of talking."**

Five questions you can't ask enough times

If you want to listen more, then one of the easiest ways to do so is to ask questions. Questions are the positive way of playing "conversational ping-pong" as they build depth to the conversation by clarifying and developing understanding.

Where great leaders separate themselves from other leaders is in leading the conversation with a question, not just using questions as a response. There are five questions a leader can't ask enough. They are:

1) What is going well for you and the operation right now?
2) What isn't going well?
3) What opportunities do you see to develop yourself and/or improve the operation?
4) What problems are you seeing/facing?
5) How can I help you do your job better?

The answers to these questions give insight and direction for the leader, employee, and operation. If you are worried the content you are listening to is only marginally important, try asking these questions and I guarantee what you hear will be worthwhile.

Keep friends close, but enemies closer

When people find themselves in a disagreement with someone, it seems like the natural tendency is to dig in your heels and start fighting for your position. This is actually the opposite of what you should do. When you disagree with someone it's important you focus on *listening better*, not speaking with more conviction. Listening more intently to their position can show you where they are wrong, where they are right, and/or what assumptions their position is based on. It is this information that is essential in proving out whether you are right or wrong. And in the case of you being right, these things will help you convince them, not just repeating yourself at higher and higher volumes. So when you disagree with someone, it's the most important time to listen as well as possible.

Making lemonade out of lemons

You can learn from anything, even bad conversations that seem like a waste of time. I don't care how dreadful the discourse is, there are any number of things you can gather.

What can you learn about the issue? Maybe you have some ideas for fixing the issue even if they don't. Perhaps you spot an opportunity that isn't being discussed. Is there background on the topic you can gather? What do you see in the report or spreadsheet?

What can you learn about the person? Are they organized? Did they prepare? Are they analytical? Logical? Do they blindly fight for their position? Are they intimidated easily? Do they get frustrated with people who don't understand? Are they capable or incapable in their role?

Idea inspiration? Sometimes a bad idea is the inspiration for great ideas. Sometimes the background you get from a report lays the foundation for a way forward on something else.

And if you don't learn anything like the above, you can at least learn patience and how to show respect. Both traits are invaluable throughout the course of your career, so while you might want something more productive from your time, being forced to practice these two traits is productive in its own right.

ROAD WORK AHEAD

The most obvious application of this principle is in meetings. The next time you find yourself in a boring or pointless meeting, don't secretly check e-mail on your phone or "zone-out." Sharpen your skills by listening more intently to the areas just discussed. You'll find that you always discover something, and it turns unproductive aspects of your day productive.

You Know the Route, Now Start Driving

What one tactic from the "Better" or "Great" will you employ now that you are done with the chapter?

What actions will you take to improve?

What date and time will you take action?

When will you review the results?

What is one other tactic you wish to employ when you are satisfied with the results of the first?

Souvenirs From The Trip

How to Be Better
It's not you, it's me
One great question for keeping the conversation about what the other person wants to get out of it, and not just what you want to get out of it.

Conversational ping-pong
Three techniques to help you listen to understand, not just listen to respond.

Let's get physical
Four ways to practice "active listening."

Please sir, could I have some more?
Why you aren't getting the whole story, and the "catch-all" question you can ask to get it.

Change the channel
Improving your listening by ensuring you are listening to all audiences.

A Pothole to Avoid
Why listening is only half of the equation.

How to Be Great
Get formal
Why great listeners have a structure to their communication, and what that structure looks like.

Find the quiet ones
The two types of quiet employees, and the feedback you should try to get from them.

Be Sherlock Holmes
Why listening isn't just about the words that are spoken, and three examples of how reading body language can enrich your listening.

Five questions you can't ask enough times
Make your listening worthwhile to both you and your audience by directing the conversation with the right questions.

Keep friends close, but enemies closer
Why a disagreement should be an invitation to listen better.

Making lemonade out of lemons
Three techniques for making the most out of a bad discussion.

"Expressways"
Go on Walkabout
Why managing by walking around can greatly improve your listening and leadership.

Enjoy The Silence
The power of keeping your mouth shut.

2.

Prioritizing

Ensure your work isn't a waste

YOU MAY NOT
BE ABLE TO
GET
**EVERYTHING
DONE,**
BUT WHAT
YOU CAN DO
IS GET THE
**IMPORTANT
THINGS
DONE.**

Are You Heading Down a Dead End?

Have you ever said, "I didn't accomplish anything I set out to do today?"

Have you ever finished something only to have your boss ask for something else instead?

Is your "To-Do List" riddled with half-completed tasks?

Are you aware of the possibility of saying "No" to something?

Does it seem like everything is a priority?

Spend Time on the Right Things

I'm sorry to be the bearer of bad news, but you will never get everything done. That's right, that To-Do list of yours will sprout new tasks just as soon as you get others off of it. It's like an endless game of "Whack-a-mole!" And this goes just as much for your employees as it does for you. Their To-Do lists fill up just as quickly as yours. Your question as a leader is whether all of you are doing the important things first.

We've all had that boss who shouts to you, "It all needs to get done" or, "It's all a top priority." Was that ever a help to you? Of course not. What often occurred in those situations is the quality of the work became rushed and substandard just so the deadline could be met. Don't be that boss. One of the most demotivating things for employees is when there aren't clear expectations and when their leader refuses to clarify them when asked.

Priorities are the foundation of time management. If you can get straight on your priorities and your employees' priorities, then you'll find you're getting not only more important work done, but more work period.

Why Leaders Take a Wrong Turn

Urgent vs. Important

There is a difference between urgent and important. Too often leaders interrupt one urgent task to deal with another urgent task, then another, and another. It's why they have so many projects and tasks in various stages of completion. Whether the urgent task is more important than finishing what they are currently working on should be a factor in prioritizing, and too often it isn't.

Furthermore, most things that are considered urgent, aren't urgent in the first place. My favorite example to use is whether the task would need to be done "right now" if the leader were away at lunch, or in a meeting? Most of the time it would wait until they got back. That red exclamation point in Microsoft Outlook doesn't always mean it needs to be handled it right away. E-mail response times aren't a badge of honor.

Mistaken belief they can do everything

If leaders or employees could do everything they needed to do in a day, the order it was done in loses some of its importance. Unfortunately, this is commonly cited as an excuse when things aren't completed, "I thought I would have time to get to it." This is also the excuse people tell themselves when they are avoiding certain tasks they don't want to do. If seven out of the ten things on the To-Do list are complete, but the three most important were neglected, how effective was that?

Think multi-tasking is the answer

Multi-tasking has its place (I love to eat and watch TV at the same time), but important work isn't it. There is this mistaken belief people can jump from task to task without any loss of efficiency or quality of work, and that just isn't the case. All leaders are forced to multi-task in today's organizational environment, but it won't be the answer to completing their tasks. In fact, it's more likely to make them more difficult.

How to Be Better

The Priority Matrix

Want to know what you should be working on? Want to know how to decide what an employee should work on first? The first thing to assess is how important and how urgent it is. It seems obvious we should be working on the most important things over less important things, but you'll have a very real temptation to do the opposite in many cases. To demonstrate this, apply all of the tasks on your To-Do list to the below matrix inspired by Stephen Covey's Time Management Grid from his book *"First Things First."*

THE PRIORITY MATRIX

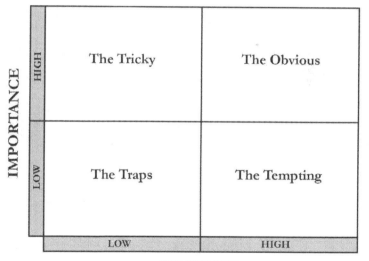

1st The Obvious – These tasks are in your face and screaming, "work on me first," and you should. If you let these tasks slip, it likely shows negatively on your performance as a leader.

2nd The Tricky – This is where self-management kicks in. You may try to trick yourself into moving these up or down on your priority list based on what you "feel" like doing.

3rd The Tempting – Where management of others comes in. You will have people asking for updates. You will have people pressuring you. This will tempt you to put these ahead of items you shouldn't, resist that temptation as much as possible. The more time you spend on high importance items, the more effective you will be.

4th The Traps – Do you want to know the secret of the low importance and low urgency items in this quadrant? They take care of themselves. Half of them go away without you doing anything; either people take them off your hands, or they weren't anything that needed to be done in the first place. The other ones get upgraded as they gain either urgency or importance with time.

For leaders, this matrix should be utilized to help you in setting priorities for your employees so you don't turn into the boss who wants everything done right now and claims they are all top priorities.

One other concept you need to take into account when considering what to work on first is priorities change. The low priority item yesterday can become your highest priority item today. Spending time reviewing priorities once a day, or once every couple of days, is one of the best uses of your time because it ensures you're making the most of all the time you have.

You're dead without deadlines

If you can't assess the urgency of a task, then it makes it far more difficult to prioritize the task. The simplest way to gauge urgency is through deadlines. If a task has been put on your plate, you need to assign it a deadline. One of the problems with deadlines is everyone knows they affect the priority of the item, so they "fiddle" with them. Sure, you would like to have it done by tomorrow, but does it really just need to get done by next week? This sort of manipulation of deadlines will cause you to spend less time working on important items. So make sure you're getting the real deadline, not a preferred deadline.

"Squirrel?!?!"

In the Pixar movie *Up* there is a talking dog, and one of the funnier aspects of the movie is getting a window into how a dog thinks. One of those is how he would immediately stop whatever he was doing at the sight or sound of a squirrel. This example relates to you and your work in that there are constant distractions and demands on your attention. When we talk about getting our priorities across the finish line, you need to spend time on your focus as well. If you cannot manage your focus, you cannot manage your time.

The essential aspect of focus is to work on just one thing at a time for as much time as you can. Most leaders don't take control over distractions. You are not required to address every issue somebody brings to your attention in the instant they do so. You are looking for as much unbroken time in your day as possible. To do this you're going to need to manage interruptions better. One of the things about interruptions is there is discretion that can be exercised by the person interrupting and the person being interrupted. If you want to maintain more focus and be interrupted less, then take control over that discretion. Don't believe me? Here's a perspective on getting 10 more minutes to finish what you're working on, and a perspective on getting an entire hour:

- 10 minutes: What if you were on a phone call, would they interrupt you?
- 60 minutes: What would they do if you were in the conference room in a meeting, or at lunch?

If you need 10 minutes to finish off what you're working on, or another 30-60 minutes, keep these two examples in mind and ask them to come back. Of course, there will be urgent items that demand an interruption, and in those cases your team would interrupt a phone call or meeting.

When an employee is interrupting your flow and focus on important items and they are insistent they need you right now, train them in this concept by asking them, "Would you interrupt me for this if I was on the phone?" No, then come back in 10 minutes (or go out and find them yourself when you're done). "Would you interrupt a meeting for this?" No, then come back in 45 minutes. These little interruption sidetrack many of your tasks and relegate them to the "partially done list." Fight them when you can.

"To achieve great things, two things are needed; **a plan, and not quite enough time"**

-Leonard Bernstein

EXPRESSWAY

Schedule your "To-do list" – With priorities and deadlines in place, it is time to start planning to accomplish as much important work within the deadlines as possible. Benjamin Franklin said, "For every minute spent organizing, an hour is earned."

The way you do this is to put each item from your task list on your calendar in 15 minute, 30 minute, 60 minute, or whatever time blocks are appropriate for completion. This helps you plan out meeting the deadlines you have set, helps you to stay focused on the priorities you have set for yourself (you won't have scheduled something that wasn't a priority) and helps limit distractions by establishing times when others can meet with you during times that are free from your priorities.

The productive procrastination myth

The two main reasons so many people fill their day with low importance and low urgency items is they are looking for a break and they are procrastinating doing the more important items on their list. There are productive distractions and unproductive ones; the productive ones help you stay focused on high priority items, and the unproductive ones keep you away from them.

Everybody needs regular breaks in their day to operate at peak efficiency. The key is to create a structure around these breaks so you control how much time you spend on them and the work you want to be doing. Two techniques for you to consider are:

The Pomodoro Technique – Developed by Francesco Cirillo in the late 1980's, you schedule 25 minutes of focused work, then a five-minute break. After four or five sessions, you take a longer break. The idea is that with the understanding of a break coming, your mind is free to focus on the task at hand. If you find yourself grinding down, then it's time for a longer break.

The Cheat Task – Similar to a "cheat day" in dieting, give yourself an allowance of one or two low/low items from the Priority Matrix every day that you allow yourself to do. The idea is for you to give yourself some structured flexibility to blow off mental steam, and then you're back to work. But just like a diet, you still need the mental toughness to see it through and get back to the higher priority items. One other caution on this, make sure you *are* giving your mind a break. Without a mental break, the cheat task is a waste.

ROAD WORK AHEAD

It's imperative to your productivity that you are focused in both your work and your break time. Both of the above techniques attempt to accomplish that. Try both of these techniques over the next two days to bring more focus on your higher priority items and see how they work for you. If there is another technique you believe could work for you, you are welcome to entertain any you feel will accomplish the result you are after.

Teach your employees to fish

You can't always be there to prioritize every single thing for your employees. The "sweet spot" for leaders isn't when your employees are following the priorities you've set, it's when they understand the thought process behind priorities and can prioritize for themselves. As the old states, "Give a man a fish and you feed him for a day; teach a man to fish and you feed him for a lifetime." The easiest way to do this is to give explanations as you're giving priorities.

- Why is it important?
- Why is it a higher priority than something else?
- Why is it a lower priority than other things?

When you can accomplish this consistently, then your employees understand the thought process behind your priorities, they understand the task better, and they get a better understanding of other tasks as well.

A Pothole to Avoid

Underestimating the time, effort, and resources necessary to complete a task or project can throw your prioritizing efforts right out the window. Leaders who are otherwise great at prioritizing, often see their efforts fail because one of their tasks takes up more time and effort than anticipated. Getting clear on the effort required, resources required, action plan, and what time is needed for things to go wrong is essential in properly prioritizing. You get ahead of this in two ways:

- If you are always planning your priorities around completing them in a "perfect world" you'll be far more likely to fail at them. Things usually take longer to complete in the real world than the one we schedule, so when working through your plan, anticipate extra time, energy and resources to be needed.

- Make sure you are clear on everything that is required for proper completion of the task. Better to ask 10 clarifying questions about what is to be delivered at the beginning of the task, than having those questions answered after you have potentially wasted effort going in the wrong direction.

Be prudent in your assessment of what is necessary to complete a task or project to keep your priorities in line. You can always fill-in your calendar with other priorities if you have extra time.

How to Be Great
* *

Well begun is half done

Did the question at the beginning of this chapter, "Have you ever said, 'I didn't accomplish anything I set out to do today?'" ring true for you? Well, if you're clear on your priorities, shouldn't you start your day with the highest priority items first? The first 30 minutes of a leader's day is one of the most mismanaged pieces of time there is. What if you didn't check e-mail when you first got in? What if you didn't discuss last night's TV show or game? What if you stopped waiting for people to bring you their priorities? Leaders are constantly placing the priority tasks of other people ahead of their own, and then wondering why they never get anything off their To-Do list. If instead you didn't open e-mail, didn't open up conversations, shut your office door and spent 30 minutes working on your highest priority item, what would that do to your productivity?

Throughout the course of every work day distractions happen, emergencies pop-up, and priorities get juggled. But those interruptions happen least in the beginning of the day. Start your day strong and you'll be more likely to carry that momentum throughout the rest of your morning and day.

ROAD WORK AHEAD

For your yourself, and your employees, another principle is to start tasks right after you receive them. Your flow has already been interrupted, so there's no better time to start the new task than when all of the deliverables are clear to you. If you can't finish it in one sitting, you at least have made tangible progress.

This is especially powerful after a meeting. Spending the first five minutes after a meeting to get your action items started, utilizes the momentum from the meeting and helps you deliver on the new task.

Buffering isn't just for videos

Nothing throws off your day like emergencies popping up out of nowhere. But are they really out of nowhere? You know you are going to get interrupted with some crisis. You know your boss is going to come to you with something that needs to get handled right away. You know one of your low priority tasks is going to suddenly blow up and become a high priority.

The way around this is to create "buffer time." This is time you set aside in your schedule for not only emergencies, but shifting priorities. It might be 30 minutes in the morning and 30 minutes in the afternoon. Just enough where you can handle something that's thrown at you. There are limits to your planning, and if you have a calendar packed with back to back meetings and tasks, then you have set yourself up for failure.

Too many leaders go through the exercise of planning, but then when an emergency comes up and they lose an hour or two, their day is thrown into chaos and they lose all sense of priority and focus. Prioritize the day and allow for some time to address emergencies. If none occur, then you simply fill in the time with an appropriate priority item.

EXPRESSWAY

You only have so many good decisions – People are able to make only so many good decisions over the course of a day. As the day wears on, and the quantity of decisions continues to climb, you encounter something known as decision fatigue. In studies conducted by Jonathan Levav of Stanford University, decision fatigue negatively affected the quality and consistency of the outcomes of anything from buying a suit or a car, to judges decisions in parole hearings. For that reason, it's best to handle your highest priority and most important items as early in your day as possible.

*Levav, Jonathan. "Extraneous factors in judicial decisions" (2011), "Decision Fatigue Saps Willpower — if We Let It" (2011)

The art of saying "No"

Highly productive people control their time and focus. Whether it is a flat out "no," or delegating the task out, you need to control what you are doing if you want to be able to control your priorities. The reason so many of us are out of balance in our personal and professional lives is we are taking the easy route and just saying "yes" to everything.

Some of the difficulties in doing so are we don't know how to say "no." Below are 10 tips for saying "no" to help you take more control over what it is you and your team are tasked with:

Realize saying "No" is OK – The first thing you need to get comfortable with is that saying "No" is OK, as long as you have a reason for it. If your reason is perceived to be insufficient by the other person, or they want more clarity, then this opens up a discussion. You don't expect a "yes" 100% of the time you ask someone to do something, and neither does the person asking you. So focus on the reason for the "no" and the other person will be more likely to go with it.

Ask for an adjustment – Maybe the due date is adjusted, maybe the scope, or maybe more resources are put behind it. There's no reason either side can't be flexible in getting something done.

Propose something else – Similar to the above is suggesting a different way of addressing the need. It could be asking someone else to do it, or coming up with a different plan. This is usually a very good idea when saying "no" anyways. Even if you can't directly help with the solution, you can help find one.

Delegate it – When you are under a time and focus crunch, it is natural to delegate. Think about how much stuff your boss gives you to do before they head out on vacation. You can take on the task, but leave the majority of the work to a member of your team and simply maintain oversight of it.

Ask for a priority change – There will be many times where a "no" isn't going to be accepted. In those cases, ask where it fits into current priorities and work. It may be if priorities are reshuffled you would have initially said "yes."

Be clear on what is a priority and say "no" to everything else – Speaking of priorities, there is a philosophy on time management that is applicable here. It states that anything that doesn't address your top three priorities shouldn't make it on your To-Do list. While this may be a bit extreme, there is a lesson there for when you should consider a "no."

Know what saying "yes" means – Too many times we may say "yes" only to figure out later the scope and effort of the task was considerably more than we expected. Don't get "buyer's remorse." Ask clarifying questions before giving an answer so you are clear on how much and what kind of work is really being sought.

Take advantage of options – There are ways to make most tasks fit cleanly into your schedule if you avail yourself of all the options. Place, time, scope, people involved, etc., are all options that can help you execute the task and turn your "no" into a "yes."

Keep your "no" simple – There is no need to belabor the "no." Leave it as a simple, "I don't think I can/should take that on, because _____." If you keep it to a simple one or two sentences you will get the discomfort for both parties over quicker and you can both move on.

Be respectful – Just like you have a reason for saying "no," the other person had a reason for bringing it to you. Respect that reason, whatever it is, by not being dismissive, offended, or angry about being asked in the first place. Listen without interrupting them while they explain. Showing them respect will help them to reciprocate and show you respect with your decision.

Managing your work and managing your life requires you to make decisions. The most important decisions relate to priorities and where you spend your time. If you can better control what's on your To-Do list, it becomes easier to prioritize. To do that, you'll need to say "no" from time to time.

"Leaders are constantly placing the **priority tasks of other people** ahead of their own, and then wondering why they **never get anything off their To-Do list.**"

Make a Starbucks run

Having trouble managing the interruptions? Need to regain your focus? Take your laptop to a conference room, to a peer's office, or to the local Starbucks and really focus on your priority items. Again, the operation survives without you when you're at lunch or a meeting, so if you need more focus, put yourself in an environment where you can get it. Of course, there are limits to how much time you should spend away. Remember, your availability to your employees is essential to their success, but getting away from your office a couple of times a week for an hour could be a huge help in getting your most important work done.

Don't sweat the wrong things

When you're working on priorities, and especially when working within each priority quadrant, it's always nice to focus on the Pareto Principle. The Pareto Principle is named after Italian economist Vilfredo Pareto and states that 80% of the output comes from 20% of the input. Whilst this is a principle, not a law of nature, it has all kinds of applications in your work when you apply it. In this case, you want to find the 20% of tasks that will get you 80% of your results to find out where your time is most productively spent.

To do this, we're going to create another matrix with importance and effort as the axis. Take all of your tasks that fell into a particular quadrant of the Priority Matrix (i.e. the High Urgency, High Importance quadrant), and plot them on the matrix.

THE 80/20 MATRIX

	LOW	HIGH
HIGH	Do First	Do Second
LOW	Do Third	Do Last

IMPORTANCE

EFFORT TO COMPLETE

High Importance & Low Effort – Do First

High Importance & High Effort – Do Second

Low Importance & Low Effort – Do Third

Low Importance & High Effort – Do Last

Now you know where you should start to get the absolute most out of your time in a particular quadrant. One way to tweak this is to reverse the second and third quadrants if you need to build some momentum with quick wins to get you through a tough spot in your day. Some may be tempted to use this matrix instead of the Priority Matrix, but I would caution against that as it does not account for deadlines and urgency.

You Know the Route, Now Start Driving

What one tactic from the "Better" or "Great" will you employ now that you are done with the chapter?

What actions will you take to improve?

What date and time will you take action?

When will you review the results?

What is one other tactic you wish to employ when you are satisfied with the results of the first?

Souvenirs From The Trip

How to Be Better
The Priority Matrix
A simple method for determining what is a priority and what isn't.

You're dead without deadlines
Why they are important, and why every task needs one for you to be able to prioritize.

"Squirrel?!?!"
A method for stopping distraction so you can gain 10-60 minutes to complete what you're working on.

The productive procrastination myth
Why breaks are important and two techniques for taking them productively.

Teach your employees to fish
Three explanations that teach your employees to prioritize for themselves.

A Pothole to Avoid
How over-achieving leaders derail their efforts to prioritize.

How to Be Great
Well begun is half done
The way to get a headstart on your day, and your tasks.

Buffering isn't just for videos

A technique that helps you stay on track, even when emergencies come up.

The art of saying "No"

10 ways it doesn't need to be as hard as you make it.

Make a Starbucks run

The "nuclear option" when you absolutely must avoid distraction.

Don't sweat the wrong things

A simple technique for making the absolute most out of the time and energy you have.

"Expressways"
Schedule your "To-do list"

The most effective way to organize your priorities.

You only have so many good decisions

Why your most important decisions should take place at the beginning of your day, not the end.

3.

Delegation

The greatest struggle and
opportunity in leadership

THE BEST "HACK" FOR BOTH TIME MANAGEMENT AND EMPLOYEE DEVELOPMENT IS **DELEGATION**

Are You Heading Down a Dead End?

If you want something done right, do you have to do it yourself?

Have your staff stopped presenting their ideas to you?

Are you drowning in work?

Do you postpone long-range projects to stay on top of short-range tasks?

Do you struggle to get your team to step up to help when needed?

Do operations slow down when you're away?

Working Through Your People

If there was one thing that could be considered a "universal struggle" amongst leaders it would be delegation. The reason delegation is such an issue is most leaders were promoted based on individual achievement. By contrast, leaders are most successful when they support the individual achievement of their employees. You achieve less yourself, but more as a group. This back and forth between focusing on individual and team achievement is a constant struggle throughout a leadership career.

One of the biggest secrets of delegation is that the most powerful benefit for you isn't in the time you save by not doing the task. Sure, it allows you more time to focus on higher priority items, but that isn't the best thing to come out of delegating. The biggest benefit of delegation is the development of your staff. When you expose them to new things you are making an investment in them. You are adding to their skillset, you are adding to their experience, and best of all, you're teaching them to stretch themselves and do more. When you can do that, you increase the value of your team to the operation.

Delegation is also a way to demonstrate that you believe in your employee's abilities, and trust them to carry out what needs to be done. The best staff in the world is useless if their leader doesn't trust them enough to give them tasks and projects that will challenge them. It's in this way that delegation can be a driver of job satisfaction and overall positive morale, in addition to all of the other benefits.

Why Leaders Take a Wrong Turn

Lack of control

As a leader, one of the most important things is control. Leaders want to be in control of themselves, their team, and what their team produces. And there's nothing wrong with that. Where leaders go wrong is when they think control means they need to do everything themselves without managing the flow of duties within the organization.

Job security

If a leader wants job security, if they want to be indispensable to the organization, then they need to produce outstanding results. If a leader is relying on hoarding knowledge, they're fooling themselves. Somebody can always learn a skill, a report, or a task. Very few people learn how to develop employees, foster teamwork, and drive results with those things.

And what's even better is that with those results they're increasing their value to the organization. If they're hoarding knowledge, they're only maintaining the status quo. Who do you think gets better raises and promotions; someone who maintains the status quo, or someone who increases the value of themselves, their people, and the organization?

"I'm an Expert"

If there isn't anybody in the department that can do a task better than the leader, then that just proves how poor of a trainer the leader is. Leaders need to have a wider focus. It's entirely likely they are misjudging both how good they are and the potential of their employees. If they don't introduce others to tasks and projects, then they just don't know.

How to Be Better
* * * * * * * * * * * * * * * * * * *

A simple step by step

Your idea of delegation might be, "Here, I need you to do this." While that may be fine for simple tasks, eventually you need to get to work on more complex tasks that won't work out well at all if that is the way you train the team.

A simple step-by-step plan for delegating any leader can follow is: "I Do, We Do, You Do." Here's the breakdown with two intermediary steps to make sure the communication is there.

I Do – It is more difficult to effectively delegate things you haven't mastered yourself. Mastering the task yourself ensures you know what you're delegating, how to teach it, evaluate it, and how to manage the final product.

I Do, You Watch – This is the employee's first exposure "behind the curtain" of how this task/project is done. Go slow and be methodical, hit the main points and go through the "why's" behind what you are doing.

We Do – Now you give them some experience working beside you, asking them questions about what to do next, and letting them do parts of the task.

You Do, I Watch – But before you just let them run with it, give them some experience working through the task/project from start to finish where you can simply observe.

You Do – Now let them go for it. Review the finished product. Ask them if they have any questions after they're done.

The reason "I Do, We Do, You Do" is so successful for delegating tasks is there is ample opportunity for communication and complete knowledge transfer. This addresses all of the questions that come up, and if there is a breakdown in the final result, there is a shared experience where the two of you can identify where the mistake was made.

EXPRESSWAY

Deadline "safety net" – Especially when initially delegating, you will often notice something with the final product that you didn't notice in the updates and/or forgot to relay in your instructions. To give yourself the time to address these issues and still be successful in meeting timelines, set your deadline ahead of the time you actually need it so you have the chance to make any final tweaks and adjustments.

Who wants it the most

Leaders often make a big mistake in delegating tasks by not giving careful consideration to whom they are delegating to. It shouldn't necessarily be the person with the most free time at the moment, or even the person who would seem naturally suited from a skillset perspective. What you want to consider is who will be motivated to do well on the task, and where you will get the best benefit from an employee development perspective.

The best people to delegate to are the ones who are most interested in learning and going the extra mile, which are typically the employees who are looking for a promotion, or those you believe have potential. Not only will they do better, you're also showing them one of the most important aspects of leadership; delegation.

ROAD WORK AHEAD

One of the best places to start for leaders who are struggling to delegate is choosing to whom they delegate. Come up with a list of three people you have the most trust to complete tasks you give them. When you come up with something you would like to delegate, make sure these are the people you delegate to first.

Starting off on the right foot

A lot of leaders stop delegating because they aren't getting the results they want quickly enough. Choosing the right things to delegate can set you up for success, or doom your efforts to failure. To get started, consider just two things related to the tasks you are considering delegating:

- Which tasks are the most frequent?
- Which tasks take longer to train than others?

Now plug the tasks into the appropriate boxes on the following matrix:

DELEGATION PRIORITY MATRIX

		FREQUENCY OF TASK (LOW)	FREQUENCY OF TASK (HIGH)
AMOUNT OF TRAINING REQUIRED	**HIGH**	**Do Last** (Focus on Other Things)	**Do Third** (Employee Development)
	LOW	**Do Second** (Delegation Practice)	**Do First** (Quick Wins)
		LOW	HIGH

FREQUENCY OF TASK

Do First (Quick Wins) – By getting these quick wins off your plate you gain back more time to be able to focus on higher priority items, and get some positive momentum behind the effort you're putting into delegating.

Do Second (Delegation Practice) – Tasks in this quadrant provide you the extra benefit of practicing delegation. As you will see, delegation is a skill like any other, and before you tackle the tasks and projects that require more investment in time and effort on your part, it's wise to get as much practice as possible.

Do Third (Employee Development) – These are probably the most important tasks to delegate as they are more involved from your standpoint and have the most impact from an employee development aspect.

Do Last (Focus on Other Things) – The only time I would look to address items in this area is if there is an outsized benefit for the development of the employee. Otherwise, your time might be better spent taking a fresh look at what is on your plate, re-ranking the items on this matrix, and beginning again.

Utilizing the above matrix ensures you are getting the most impact from your time delegating.

Not just for your teeth

Control matters, but it's control over the finished product that matters most. If you want to maintain control while not doing all of the work, one of the simplest ways to do so is to schedule regular check-ups. It can either be you going to the employee or them coming to you. These checkups are your chance to be comfortable with the progress from a timeliness and a quality standpoint. If adjustments need to be made, you can do them here.

If you struggle with trusting your employees to do the work you want them to do, using check-ups on tasks you delegate is a great way to build confidence and trust in your team by giving them a chance to produce without you, yet still be able to instruct them.

Recognize!

If you want to have an easier time delegating, don't forget to grease the wheels with a hefty dose of appreciation. Saying "thanks" when the task is complete ensures you're great at delegating from start to finish, and builds the confidence of the employee to handle more tasks in the future. So when you've handed off a task and it's been done well, make sure you celebrate the extra effort and the good work the employee put into it. This is an investment in the future motivation they will have to help out, to learn, and to grow.

"Delegation requires the willingness to pay for short term failures

in order to gain long term competency."

~Dave Ramsey

A Pothole to Avoid

One of the ways leaders fail in delegation is that they procrastinate delegating tasks until they "have to" because their plate is full. If they have the time to do the task over the normal course of their day, they figure that they will just do it and get it done. The problem with this thinking is that you are less likely to set up the employee whom you are delegating to for success. Your plate is full, you don't have as much time to teach them what you really need to, you can't answer questions, and the task itself is more likely to already be behind schedule, thus setting them up to miss the deadline. You need to make choices that make sense when you have the option of being effective. Waiting until you have no choice but to delegate is likely to get far worse results for you than if you had done it when you first recognized it as an option.

How to Be Great

Don't sabotage it

You may have tried to delegate over the last few months and you may have failed, or it may be it just seems to be more of a struggle than it needs to be. Before you put these failures on the skillsets or attitudes of your team, make sure you haven't inadvertently sabotaged your delegation efforts.

Now you may be saying, "Cameron, why would I sabotage it, I know it's the right thing to do?" But it's not just about what you know. As with many things in leadership, emotions play into it as well. You may subconsciously still be uncomfortable with it, concerned about how others will perceive it, or just not convinced you're doing your job right if you hand things off.

When you find the results of your delegation efforts falling short of expectations, take a look in the mirror and see if any of these issues have come up:

Holding back information – In a rush for more time, are you leaving out important details on how you want a task done, or what the final product should look like? Have you said, "Just do it" when delegating duties?

Perfectionist – If you are always finding fault in what you give people to do, they'll stop giving their best effort because it doesn't matter whether they do or not. Hyper-focusing on the minutiae and not the bigger picture is a recipe for demotivating your staff instead of developing them.

Disappearing – If they have questions, are you there to answer them, or are you in meetings, out of the office, behind closed doors, or too busy to help them? Questions come up over the course of even routine tasks, let alone something new. If you disappear and offer no support, no wonder you aren't getting the results you want.

Time and resources – You need to allot time not only for the task, but also the learning curve the employee will inevitably have to go through. Similarly, we don't always realize what goes into accomplishing the task, and the resources we have available as leaders.

Authority – Beyond resources is authority. Especially when the delegated task or project requires the collaboration of peers or other departments. A subordinate needs to get clear authority to "speak on your behalf." If you don't set the authority ahead of time, they could get stymied in questions of why they are asking others for things, and why it's more important than other duties.

Make sure you are doing everything you can to set up your employees for success in delegation and you don't unwittingly sabotage your own efforts.

Delegate up and sideways

Most people think only of delegating down the chain of command, but there's no reason you shouldn't delegate to your boss or peer when appropriate. The reason: delegation is about getting the most out of everyone's time and experience for the benefit of the organization. Delegation allows you to ensure everyone is working within their strengths; you, your employees, and your boss. There may be a task that takes you three hours to do, that a peer could do in 30 minutes. Likewise, there may be a task that is *far* more likely to be successful if your boss took over.

Now let me address the thought that immediately comes to your mind: Doesn't that hamper my development? Yes, it does in regards to the particular task, but that doesn't mean you can't be using the extra time and energy to develop yourself even more in another area.

So how do you make the pivot to delegating to a peer, or heaven forbid, your boss? Keep these things in mind:

Explain why – If you can explain to a peer or boss why it would be much quicker, more efficient, and more successful for them to do it than you, then it makes sense.

Offer to take something off of their plate – Quid pro quo (this for that). If you are delegating something to them, it follows that you should return the favor and take something off of their plate. When doing this it's important you are sure of the quality you will bring to the task (it does no good if they need to spend time reworking it). Also, make sure you're taking *more* than you are asking them to take on, this makes it a win-win proposition for both of you.

Ask for help if they don't agree – Even if they say no, it doesn't mean you can't ask for their help with the task so that perhaps you can learn and be able to do it better next time.

There are a ton of legitimate reasons why a peer or boss may turn you down. The most common would be they have bigger issues to deal with and don't have the time or attention for it, or can't delegate anything on their plate to do a trade for time. Those who truly master delegation can identify opportunities everywhere to smooth the whole operation and improve the productivity of everyone.

EXPRESSWAY

What happens when you're on vacation? – Make a list of the tasks that wait until you come back, and which ones are handled by someone else in your absence. Note who handles those tasks. These may be areas where you can consider yourself "always on vacation," and take them off your plate completely. This exercise also addresses who you can delegate to.

"Delegation allows you to ensure that everyone is working within their strengths; you, your employees, and your boss."

Spring cleaning

Just because you have delegated a task or responsibility does not mean your responsibility for continuously improving that area goes away. One of the powers of delegating is you are able to look at a task or responsibility from a new perspective, but with all of the knowledge you already have from being in the trenches actually doing it. The questions to ask generally fall into three main categories:

- *How can it be done quicker?* Are there ways to automate some steps to speed up the process of completion now that you aren't actually doing the work? Is it possible some steps be eliminated?
- *How can it be done easier?* Are there forms that can be filled out? Can you create a checklist? Are there ways to give the task more clarity and visibility?
- *How can you increase its impact?* Are there simple things that can be added to increase its usefulness to your department? To other departments?

Your focus initially needs to be squarely on seeing that what you have delegated is of the quality you expect, but once you have that assurance in place, then you can transition to making it better.

Want to take this concept to the next level? Have the employee who you have delegated the task to answer the three questions as well. You might be surprised at what a "fresh pair of eyes" sees, and it's a way to further you delegation and the empowerment of your team.

Don't eat the frog, pass it along

Brian Tracy coined the term, "Eat the frog" to describe the time management tactic of doing the task you dread the most as soon as possible. While I absolutely love this time management technique, I also believe it presents an opportunity for you to kick start the satisfaction you get out of delegating. Instead of "eating the frog", why not delegate it to one of your employees to do.

This won't work with every task you dislike; many are tasks you must handle yourself for a number of viable reasons. But where possible, see if you can train someone else to do it. What is a "frog" to you, may be a welcome challenge for an employee, and part of the reason it may be better to do so is the fact that if you dislike doing a task, there is a fair chance you aren't doing it as well as you should. It may be that the "frog" not only gives you practice delegating and your employee some empowerment, it may just turn out better in general.

You Know the Route, Now Start Driving

What one tactic from the "Better" or "Great" will you employ now that you are done with the chapter?

What actions will you take to improve?

What date and time will you take action?

When will you review the results?

What is one other tactic you wish to employ when you are satisfied with the results of the first?

Souvenirs From The Trip

How to Be Better
A simple step by step
A five step process to ensure that everyone is as clear as possible on the delegated task.

Who wants it the most
Where to find the employees who will be excited to take on a delegated task.

Starting off on the right foot
The simple technique for picking what tasks to delegate first.

Not just for your teeth
How you can maintain control through updates.

Recognize!
Why your job isn't done when the delegated job is done.

A Pothole to Avoid
How procrastinating on delegating can doom it to failure

How to Be Great
Don't sabotage it
Five things to guard against so that you don't undermine all of your effort.

Delegate up and sideways
How to delegate to your peers and boss for the benefit of everyone.

Spring cleaning

The critical step to delegation almost every leader misses.

Don't eat the frog, pass it along

A great place to start delegating, and insurance you aren't doing the bare minimum on your tasks.

"Expressways"

Deadline "safety net"

The most important thing to account for in the learning curve of your employees

What happens when you're on vacation?

You're already delegating more than you know.

4.

Communication

The prerequisite for success

THE QUALITY OF THE RESULTS YOU ARE LOOKING FOR **WILL MATCH THE QUALITY OF YOUR COMMUNICATION.** IF YOU WANT BETTER RESULTS, **GET BETTER AT COMMUNICATING.**

Are You Heading Down a Dead End?

How many times has somebody taken a text you wrote in the wrong way?

Are you hearing about bad news too late?

Are people avoiding eye contact or not paying attention when you speak?

Is work coming back to you differently than what you'd envisioned?

Have you been caught up in a conference call or an e-mail stream where nobody seems to be understanding what anyone else is talking about?

Are your directions taken by your employees without any clarifying questions, dialogue, or conversation?

A Hidden Driver of Performance

Today is the Information Age, and all of the answers we want are usually just a Google search away. That level of communication, transparency, and insight flows into every area of our lives. For leaders, this means communication with their teams is more of a requirement now than it ever has been. Your people expect it and crave it. And that's great, because communication is one of the primary traits of strongly performing organizations.

Your leadership will rise or fall based on your ability to communicate. It is the means by which ideas are shared, teams are aligned toward the same goals, performance feedback is given both up and down the organizational hierarchy, and above all it clarifies what is occurring and what is needed. To be a great leader, you can't take your communication and the disseminating of information for granted, because when you improve or regress in your skills in this area, your career and performance follows suit.

Why Leaders Take a Wrong Turn

Think they're better than they are

Almost everybody thinks they communicate well. After all, leaders always understand what they mean, what is implied, and all of the details when they communicate. The issue is communication isn't about them, it's about them *and* their audience. Leaders routinely don't:

- Give enough context
- Give enough clarity on the details
- Give out enough information at all

It's the last point that cures many of the other ills and leads to the cure for so many misperceptions people may have on their leadership. As a leader, if you don't feel like you are over-communicating, you probably aren't communicating nearly enough.

No structure

Regularly scheduled pre-shift meeting, weekly updates, one-on-one meetings, quarterly team meetings, etc. for the backbone of a good communication plan. Not having a structure for communication that holds a leader accountable for communicating at particular times is a huge red flag. The simple reason is if a structure isn't in place, then communication is dependent on priorities. If there is an emergency, crisis, or just something else that needs to be done, communication can easily take a back seat. The two most common excuses to not have a structure for communication are:

Obligation – One of a leader's best friends is flexibility. When they have flexible deadlines, employees, and responsibilities they have control over their time. Having scheduled and structured communication tasks eliminates the flexibility they may have over their time and tasks.

"No need" – Many times leaders will say they communicate when necessary and there's no need to "bloat" everyone's schedule with things can be handled in the moment. Of course, that logic would require things to be communicated in the moment, and too many times they are not.

Rushing it

One of the biggest places leaders fail at communication is they see it as an area where they can gain back time over the course of their busy days. This leaves them rushing through their communication and leaving it incomplete. Talking as they are running out the door, telling employees to start working on it and they'll come back and fill in the details, and never asking if the employee has any questions about what was asked of them.

Just as bad is when they choose to use the wrong channel for communication to speed things along, i.e. using e-mail when a phone call or in-person discussion is more appropriate. This is mis-prioritizing the content at best, and just plain lazy leadership at worst.

How to Be Better

You communicate with your ears

Real communication isn't just about you getting your point across, it's about getting the right point across in the right way. To do that you need to listen. We spent a whole chapter on it, so I won't belabor all of the tips and thoughts surrounding it, but listening holds critical value for your speaking. Listening helps you ensure you've got your point across. Listening helps you get to the heart of another person's argument. And listening helps you see the differences in how individuals communicate so you can get your point across in a way they'll understand. Listening well ensures you aren't wasting the words and thoughts you are communicating. Two concepts to show the communication flow and where listening comes in:

Listen so people will talk – The best listeners actually encourage the other person to talk more. All of the elements of active listening, coupled with questions, ensure you get as much information as possible.

Talk so people will listen – You are communicating well when what you're saying leads to people asking great questions. That often happens most when you are phrasing things in ways that are meaningful to them, not just meaningful to you.

Keep an eye on your listening skills for they truly are the foundation for your communication.

The "Communication Ladder"

Choosing the right method of communication can be just as important as what you are saying. Have you ever had something misunderstood when you e-mailed it? I bet if you had spoken with the person on the phone and said almost the exact same words, it wouldn't have been misunderstood. The "Communication Ladder" is a simple framework for identifying and adjusting the appropriate communication methods based on their importance, complexity and how emotionally charged they are:

The quality and depth of communication flows like this:

- E-mail is better than texting
- Skype is better than e-mail
- Phone calls are better than Skype
- In person is better than a phone call

Are you having a problem getting your point across, or the other person took offense to something? Move up the ladder to a better communication style. Is what you are asking very simple and straightforward? Save yourself some time and move down the ladder to a quicker communication style. Finding yourself frustrated with someone's e-mail? Don't e-mail them back, talk it out with them over the phone and put the issue to rest once and for all.

THE COMMUNICATION LADDER

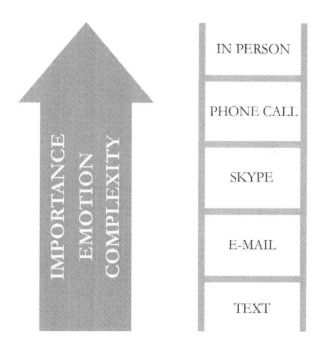

We all have our preferred communication techniques, but that preference isn't suited to every single situation. Adding flexibility into your methods of communication will help you in a number of ways:

What's the purpose – If it is something you feel is important then it is best to move up the ladder. If it is more routine or trivial, then moving down the ladder is warranted.

Relationship management – Moving up the ladder helps you add depth to your communication. Finding yourself in a strained relationship with someone? Move your communications up the ladder to both limit misperceptions and to help heal the relationship.

Are you getting the point across – If you feel like you're not getting the results you are looking for, then move up the ladder when addressing that area.

Emotions – One of the cardinal rules of e-mail is "don't e-mail emotions." I absolutely agree with that. Depending on how emotionally charged an issue is determines the best method of communicating it.

Mold to communication styles and needs – This doesn't mean that the "Communication Ladder" should be applied without flexibility. Some people are intimidated by face to face communication. Other people can't stand texting. To communicate effectively you need to understand some of these dynamics and adjust as needed to get your point across and open up a dialogue. There will also be times where you need a traceable form of communication for task management or accountability.

Technology is absolutely amazing, but to get the most out of it you need to manage how you use it. Simply keeping the "Communication Ladder" in mind as you go through your day can be a great way to help with that management.

ROAD WORK AHEAD

One of the most powerful areas that can be addressed with the "Communication Ladder" is relationships. Is there somebody you work with whom you have a strained relationship, or who just seems to take things the wrong way when you present them? Move your communication with them up one rung of the ladder for the next week. It may not solve it, but see if it improves.

"You are communicating well when what you're saying **leads to people asking great questions.**"

Tall buildings have a framework, so should your communication

Creating a structure for your communication can help you stay on track when emergencies and priorities threaten to encroach on it. Remember, communication needs to be a priority, as it ensures you are being productive with the right things and are as efficient as possible. Putting the below structure in place can help you stay on track and ensures you are getting a wide variety of feedback across varied communication forums:

One on One Meetings – (frequency: every week to every month) – If you don't have these on your calendar for at least once every couple of weeks, you are missing out on one of the most effective tools of leadership. Now I know what you're saying, "I don't have time to meet with my team every week." But guess what? You don't need nearly as much time as you think. See, once you start communicating more, you understand each other better, you've covered issues already, and you are able to communicate more efficiently. The first one-on-one that took 45 minutes, often takes 15 minutes or less from that point forward.

It can't be stated enough how much these sessions help build a bond between leader and employee, are a critical source of ideas and feedback, and are a great forum for reinforcing the vision of the organization.

So what do you go over in your one-on-ones?

Many one-on-ones suffer from the leader trying to get their point across instead of as a tool for the leader to gather valuable information and foster collaboration between themselves and the employee. To do that I recommend the below basic agenda. You'll notice it borrows heavily on the questions from Chapter 1 on listening:

1. Review of action items from last meeting.
2. What is going well for you and the operation right now?

3. What isn't going well?
4. What opportunities do you see to develop yourself and/or improve the operation?
5. What problems are you seeing/facing?
6. How can I help you do your job better?
7. What are we going to work on between now and the next meeting?

Try to talk less and question more, and your one-on-ones will be some of the most valuable hours of your week.

Team Meetings – (frequency: every month to every quarter) – These meetings are excellent opportunities to discuss the vision for the organization, build some togetherness and teamwork, get brainstorming sessions going (ideas tend to foster other ideas as your employees listen to each other), and get buy-in from the whole team on initiatives moving forward.

These aren't just sessions for you to give updates, these are sessions for you to get feedback from the team. Things that employees may not have the confidence to bring up in a one-on-one may come out more frequently when they have the back-up of teammates.

As a general rule you want to include just as many questions or feedback opportunities as you have updates. This will require you get good at mediating discussions and keeping the meeting on track, but if you can accomplish that, team meetings will become less about updates and more about moving forward together.

Put it on the board – (frequency: daily to weekly) Do you want to know how your employees know when you're really serious about something? When you're always talking about it. The funny thing is that one of the best ways in the workplace to highlight this isn't through talking at all, it's putting something up on a wall for everyone to see. Daily sales performance, daily orders shipped, customer compliment letters, etc.

Utilizing a bulletin board to constantly reinforce your priorities is communicating in a powerful way because it is public, and public things make you and everyone else accountable. It is also just one more communication method you can utilize for those who want to read memos, meeting minutes, or the results of the latest customer survey instead of hearing about them through some other means.

EXPRESSWAY

The best response – If you want to foster more open communication with your employees, one of the best ways is through asking the right questions and sincerely listening to the responses. We talked in the chapter on Listening about the five questions you should constantly be leading out with in conversation, but what about responses? To immediately open the gates of communication, respond as often as you can with:

What do you think we should do?

This develops your employee by forcing them to be solution focused, shows them you value their opinion, and it gives you a chance to communicate with them more than if you just gave them the answer.

Get informal

Here's a simple concept most leaders don't realize; if you don't feel like you are over-communicating with your team, then you likely aren't communicating nearly enough. The reason is people aren't often great at communicating. That goes for you, and it goes for your staff as well.

The more opportunities you give yourself and your employees to communicate with each other, the better the chances are you will be communicating all of the issues, details, and thoughts you want to. This can mean walking around and saying "Hi" in the morning, checking up on everybody and seeing if they need anything during the middle of the day, asking how the day was as they leave, in the break room, after meetings, anywhere and everywhere.

Backing up a structured system of communicating with an unstructured system fills in the holes that may occur when communicating in either forum.

A Pothole to Avoid

Indulging in gossip will undermine your ability to communicate with your team faster than almost anything. It may seem like a simple route to establish rapport, but its downside is enormous. Gossip not only ruins reputations but also erodes trust. If you are willing to gossip and speculate with some employees, it begs the question of whether you gossip and speculate about all employees. Leave no place for gossip, innuendo, or speculation if you want to be respected and trusted as a communicator.

How to Be Great

Connect emotionally

Maya Angelou said it best, "People will forget what you said and did, but they will never forget how you made them feel." Great communicators are invested in the person they are communicating with, and direct their communication to address the wants, needs, and desires of that person.

Before you begin communicating, ask yourself what the other person wants out of this conversation? Ask what the emotional result is of what you are about to say? And as you move through the conversation, ask yourself how you can be a part of the plan moving forward? When you tie your actions to the actions of another, you form a bond that demonstrates how valuable they are to you. It was Theodore Roosevelt who said, "Nobody cares how much you know, until they know how much you care."

They aren't robots

Do you speak to your close friends in the same way you speak to your parents? Do you speak to your spouse the same way you do the grocery store clerk? Probably not.

Every person on your team is different, so why would you think you could communicate with them in the same way? Sure, there will be times the group e-mail works fine, but there will be just as many times you're making a compromise with time.

One of the ways to improve your conversation is to see through the perspective of others. Each of your employees has their own insecurities and values, and taking those into consideration helps you get buy-in, and limits the "friction" that might come about due to what you are saying.

"The single biggest problem in communication is the illusion that it has taken place."

~George Bernard Shaw

Why, why, why

There is one particular area of how to convey ideas and give direction that is often overlooked, but is vitally important. It is "the why." I'm not talking about you asking your team why something happened or why they did something, I'm talking about three specific things:

- Explaining why you are making the decision you are making.
- Explaining why something you are asking them to do is important.
- Explaining why you are asking them specifically to do something.

In an effort to work efficiently, leaders often assign tasks and make demands with as little context as possible. This can be detrimentally short sighted. Addressing "the why" can:

Help with understanding – When you receive back work that isn't what you were looking for, it is often an issue of context. Why you are doing something and why you assigned it to them helps eliminate the "grey area" of understanding for the employee. It fills in the blanks of your instructions and lets them take extra steps as they see necessary to give you what you want.

Give meaning to work – The primary ingredient to passion in the workplace is purpose. If you are wrapping tasks and duties around the reason they are important, then your team will understand where they personally fit within the organization.

Add transparency – In the information age we live in, people expect to understand all facets of situations. If you don't give them the reason behind your actions they will seek to fill in the blanks themselves. This can lead to all sorts of rumors and inhibitors to productivity. If you explain your actions, then you get at the root of your team's need for more information.

Help with Employee Development – When you give them insight into how you are making decisions, assigning tasks, and handling your responsibilities you are teaching them. The long term benefit of explaining "the why" is you develop your employees. This will help them address future situations in the way you want them to without your intervention.

"Grab Bag" of communication tricks

I know you may have been hoping for some simple tricks to improve your communication, and while these may not actually be simple, there are some concepts to keep in mind that can really improve the way you communicate with others:

Emphasize similarities – When I worked in the hospitality industry, one of the most effective ways for me to defuse an explosive situation with a guest was to simply say, "If I were you, I'd be just as upset, if not even more so." It showed understanding of the situation and changed us from adversaries to teammates. People are naturally attracted to people who share the same background and opinions. One way to get heard more and to get people to open up is to find similarities and bring them up in conversation.

Use people's names – Everybody's favorite word is their own name. Not only that, it makes them feel like the surrounding conversation is tailored solely to them. Don't be weird about it, but working it into the conversation can help ease tension and build the rapport between you and the other person.

Anticipate confusion – You likely know when a situation will be difficult for the other person to grasp (if you really think about it). Being prepared to move up the "Communication Ladder," or provide additional information and resources will help you get through to the other person.

Read body language – One of the reasons looking directly at the other person is so important in communication is it is not only polite and encourages them to focus on you, but it can give you ideas on how they are reacting. Are they uncomfortable and leaning toward the door, are they engaged and leaning forward, are they rolling their eyes, are they nodding in understanding or do they have a blank expression on their face?

You may already be employing some of these in your communication already, but they are all great ways to add a little extra to what you're saying.

EXPRESSWAY

Work in an empty cubicle – Working on your own work while being alongside your team for just a few hours a week will expose you to common frustrations, possible improvements, and insight into general productivity that you wouldn't get anywhere else.

But it isn't just about overhearing what is going on; it's just as much about being more accessible to them in the moment. You'd be surprised the questions you may get when there isn't any barrier at all between you and your employees.

Delivering the news

Would you treat the exceeding of quarterly sales goals in the same way you would treat layoffs? Great communicators adjust their delivery of good news and bad news based on the outcomes they are looking for. Let me show you how:

The Keys to Giving Bad News

Always in person – You want to get as far up the "Communication Ladder" as possible in order to make sure the other party is as clear as possible on the issue with no misunderstanding and the ability to ask all the clarifying questions they want. And just as important, so you can see and hear if they "get it."

Always as quickly as possible – It was Colin Powell who said, "Bad news isn't wine, it doesn't improve with age." Giving it quickly ensures they don't find out from someone else. If that is the case, you lose the ability to tailor the message, and risk having important things being left out.

Always let them know what you are doing about it – People generally have a great fear of the unknown. If you can let them know what the overall plan is moving forward, and the next step to take, you focus them on action instead of dwelling.

The idea is that you act quickly, take ownership, and plan the way out. Your plan is to be so complete and honest in your delivery of the information there is nothing left to discuss, there is just action on the plan going forward.

The Keys to Giving Good News

Bad news is something we are all used to managing, but what about the good news? Good news should be leveraged to maximize the positive benefit on your department.

Shout it from the rooftops – Make a big announcement, call it out in pre-shift, do something to make everyone aware of what took place. If you can't be sure 100% of your staff is going to know about it, you aren't "shouting" loud enough.

Pictures/Graphs – Not everyone responds to speeches or memos, or words for that matter. Really show the impact of the improvement by creating a pie chart, a graph, pictures, something.

"Own" your successes – Too often we expect the success to happen, so we don't publicize it, or we feel like we are bragging. Own them so you create the environment of positivity.

Leverage the past success for the next success – Bring your team to the next level. A positive message should always end with what is next on the horizon to strive for. This uses the success to create momentum in the operation.

While some of the elements of great communication apply to both bad news and good news, the outcome you desire is very different. Tailoring your communication to maximize the benefit and minimize the downside is essential for great communication.

ROAD WORK AHEAD

Is there a piece of good news that occurred over the last week that you didn't bother to tell your team about? Exercise your good news delivery by "shouting it from the rooftops" and including some form of graph or picture to highlight it even further. The more you practice communicating good news, the easier it becomes and the more interested your employees will be in listening to all of the news you have.

You Know the Route, Now Start Driving

What one tactic from the "Better" or "Great" will you employ now that you are done with the chapter?

What actions will you take to improve?

What date and time will you take action?

When will you review the results?

What is one other tactic you wish to employ when you are satisfied with the results of the first?

Souvenirs From The Trip

How to Be Better
You communicate with your ears
Why listening ensures you don't waste your communication.

The "Communication Ladder"
A simple method for determining the communication method you use in a particular situation.

Tall buildings have a framework, so should your communication
How scheduled communication can help hold you accountable, and the key facets of each type.

Get informal
Why it's important to give people as many chances as possible to talk with you.

A Pothole to Avoid
The one thing that can derail all of your communication efforts.

How to Be Great
Connect emotionally
What you need to ask yourself before you communicate with someone.

They aren't robots
Why acknowledging different communication styles in your team can improve how you engage your team.

Why, why, why
Building understanding one explanation at a time.

"Grab Bag" of communication tricks
Four tricks that all great communicators leverage.

Delivering the news
Why it matters how you give good news and bad news, and the key things that make the difference.

"Expressways"
The best response
The one question that encourages open communication more than almost any other.

Work in an empty cube
Why your physical location can kick your communication into high gear.

5

Micromanagement

When control is counter
productive

THE BEST
WAY TO
CONTROL
YOUR
OPERATION
IS THROUGH
OVERSIGHT,
NOT BY
DOING EVERY
JOB YOURSELF

Are You Heading Down a Dead End?

Do you feel the need to "check-in" when you're away from the office?

Do you always find something wrong with your employee's work, even if it is a small detail?

Do you take tasks back after you've delegated them?

Are your employees taking no initiative?

Have you asked to be cc'd on emails?

Do you often feel frustrated because you would've gone about a task differently?

Does your team actively avoid you?

The "Helicopter" Boss

There is a term I heard recently related to micromanaging leaders called the "Helicopter Boss." It's a play on the tendency of some bosses to hover over their employees while they are doing their work. While I think it is an amusing term, micromanagement in the workplace is anything but amusing for a leader's career. After you get done delegating, it is common to be pulled into the second most common leadership pitfall; Micromanagement. Both delegation and micromanagement are about control over the output of your team. One internalizes control and one pushes the control outward, but both are detrimental to your team's performance through their negative effect on empowerment, development, and morale.

And make no mistake micromanagement is prevalent. A survey conducted by Trinity Solutions and published in author Harry Chambers' book *My Way or the Highway* showed that 79 percent of respondents had experienced micromanagement. Approximately 69 percent said they considered changing jobs because of micromanagement and another 36 percent actually changed jobs. Seventy-one percent said being micromanaged interfered with their job performance while 85 percent said their morale was negatively impacted.

The reason micromanagement is viewed so clearly in the negative by the employee is it undermines their feeling of self-worth and their contribution being made to the organization. They may wonder why nothing they do is good enough, why you won't let them do their jobs, and the ultimate bad question; "why did you hire me?" If you can get past your own tendency to micromanage, you can get ahead of all of these and separate yourself from other leaders.

Why Leaders Take a Wrong Turn

Controlling everything

If you ask 10 people what micromanagement is really about, the number one answer will almost surely be control. Leaders are ultimately responsible for the output of their team, but they often mistakenly believe the responsibility requires that they control every aspect of this output instead of just the final result.

Nobody will do anything if I'm not there

At its best, this reasoning gets at a sense of hubris where the leader has made themselves vital to the organization. At its worst, this is an indictment of their leadership and ability to motivate and develop a team. If nothing is done without their involvement, they aren't a leader at all.

Misplaced belief they're saving time

A micromanaging leader will often mention their contribution to the task as justification for their involvement. Sure, they may have provided some valuable feedback, and they may even have helped speed the task along to completion, but this line of thinking completely ignores the fact it was two people working on the task, not one. How much other work could the leader have done on their own? How much more important work? While one task may have been done quicker, another task was slowed down.

Misplaced belief it is too important to screw up

The other common refrain from a micromanaging boss is that the task is just too important to leave any margin for mistake. Even assuming this is the case (which it usually isn't), this ignores all of the other ways a leader can assure the task is done well without them hovering over the person doing the task.

How to Be Better

Are you on schedule?

One of the first steps in conquering micromanagement is actually embracing the tendency and managing it. Instead of constantly hounding your team for updates and progress, or even worse, hovering over them while they do a task, why not set up a schedule for them to come update you?

Time Updates – Think of it like regular maintenance on your car. At certain pre-determined time periods throughout the course of the task you have the person come to you, *not* you going to them, and you can check on progress to ensure it is where you think it should be from a timeliness, scope, and quality perspective.

Toll-Gates – These are similar to updates, but instead of being based on time they are based on project milestones. It may do you no good to review progress when a step of the process is half done. If you set up a review at certain critical points, where again, the employee comes to you instead of you going to them, you can keep the project on track.

In both of these cases, the idea is to limit the updates as much as possible to ensure the work gets done effectively, but you are still kept aware of the progress.

Hitting the learning curve(ball)

When leaders mention that nothing will get done well if they aren't involved, they are simply acknowledging their failure as a teacher. In many of these cases, it isn't that they can't teach, it's more their unwillingness to go through the pain of the learning curve with their team.

No matter how capable your team is, or how great you are at instructing and developing them, there's always a learning curve for activities. Sometimes it's difficult to reconcile this with the work you need done, the quality you need for it, and the timeframe you need it completed by. Luckily there are a few things you can work on that will help you speed through the learning curve as easily as possible:

Extra time – It may not be a luxury in all cases, but where you can find the extra time, give it. With new tasks, it is natural for employees to second-guess themselves, they haven't found all of the shortcuts yet, and they have questions. The best developmental tool is struggle and failure, so it pays off towards quicker learning to be able to give them some extra time to sort through it themselves.

If you don't have the extra time, you can always direct where their learning will come from by overseeing certain aspects and letting them struggle and learn from others.

Extra support – Even if you allow them extra time, you will likely still need to be there. The best way to be there is through regular updates, not constant hovering. Another way of supporting them without micromanaging them is to assign an employee whom you trust to act on your behalf to help them when needed.

The "Why" – Probably the best thing you can do for your employees to speed the learning curve is to go deeper into the task itself. Why is it important? Why are you asking them to do it? Why does it fit into the goals of the department? This gives them the background for the task which helps them assess the priority, fill in the blanks in what you instructed them, and points them in the direction of other resources and answers.

If you are confident in what your team will give you, as well as how they are going to do it, you will be far less likely to micromanage them. The issue is getting them to that point. Work on their learning curves, acknowledge they exist and the effect they have on their performance, and get to work addressing them.

EXPRESSWAY

Examples – Whenever possible, give your team examples of what you want the final result of their task to look like. They can use this as a guide so that you need not "manage" the process, and you have the assurance of what their final product is going to look like. Use examples as often as possible in leadership to make sure everyone is clear on what you're asking.

"The best executive is one who has sense enough to pick good people to do what they want done, **and self-restraint enough to keep from meddling with them while they do it.**"

~Theodore Roosevelt

"What" not "How"

One thing that leads to a lot of micromanagement is when you not only tell an employee what to do, but also get into depth on how to do it. The key thing to remember is that you are ultimately responsible for and need to control the *final product*. General George Patton once said, "Never tell people how to do things. Tell them what to do and they will surprise you with their ingenuity." How it gets to that final stage is where you have flexibility through processes, procedures, checklists, oversight, reviews, etc. Great leaders leverage as many of these as possible so there are no bottlenecks in the operation. And if you're micromanaging, you're a bottleneck.

ROAD WORK AHEAD

One way to start practicing this is to give them the "what" and then ask them "how" they would do it? This gives you some control or reassurance as to their next steps, but it lets them come up with the plan, instead of you offering up your plan first. As long as their plan seems like it will accomplish the end result, let them run with it.

No touching the "finishing touches"

Another way leaders "cheat" their way into becoming micromanagers is by placing themselves into the process at the end. The idea is that there are certain parts of the task that would just take too long to explain to the employee, or that are somehow sensitive in nature, or don't have hard and fast parameters. The problem is once you start down this road, it's easy to keep going down the road and take back more and more aspects.

So if you have some of those tasks where you have inserted yourself at the end, then take the time to explain what it is you are doing as clearly as possible to be able to empower the employee fully.

Reminisce about your last vacation

What happened to the department the last time you took a vacation? It can be instructive for the micromanaging leader to realize the team can survive (and often thrive) without them. Look back at what specific tasks your employees were able to take over to give yourself a level of trust in their work. Look back at what they couldn't do, and instead of micromanaging it, use it as a template for what needs to be trained in the coming weeks.

A Pothole to Avoid

There will always be something "wrong" if you look hard enough. One of the worst places to micromanage, and yet one of the places that is seemingly the most natural place to do so is when evaluating employee performance. Getting into the details of how they go about their day may seem great, but it can lend itself to the concept of, "Not being able to see the forest through the trees." Evaluating how someone goes through the simplest and smallest functions of their job encourages you to undermine the natural flow of how they do the work. Instead of looking at their results (the forest), you micromanage how they get those results (the trees). Again, this may seem like a reasonable way to further improve, but if it isn't balanced with the bigger picture, it can be demoralizing and counterproductive.

How to Be Great

Stop playing dodgeball with performance

One of the biggest lies leaders tell themselves is the only way things can get done is to stay on top of their employees. One of the main reasons you "stay on top of" an employee's job is when they can't handle it; when they are late with their work, when their work is substandard, when they aren't good at delivering bad news to a customer, when their reports aren't correct, and when they lack certain skills. When they just aren't as good at their job as they should be.

In these cases, your micromanagement is actually a method of procrastinating and avoiding what you probably should be doing, which is having an honest performance appraisal with the employee and getting them the training and support they need. You are taking the "easy" way out.

Before we get into identifying some of these areas, I wanted to review some basics of leadership that support the performance of your team. It may be you are micromanaging to address performance shortfalls you helped create:

Be clear on deliverables – One of the ways leaders passively micromanage is by giving "fuzzy" direction to their team. Do you have a specific timeline? Is the employee clear on the anticipated result of their work? If you dropped the ball on either of these, you may find you need to jump in to get the task completed.

Set reasonable expectations – Then you need to ask them if what you have asked is reasonable. Note I didn't say you decide what is reasonable. Giving them a say not only helps you identify obstacles so you can address them with more time, resources, support, etc., but also empowers the employee and helps give them ownership over the process.

Support the team with training – If you aren't comfortable with whether they can meet your expectations, then this is your red flag you need to start training.

Usually discussions of micromanagement center on control, empowerment, and trust, but often the reason your team is not meeting your expectations is you need to find a way to "train them up."

ROAD WORK AHEAD

Who do you feel you micromanage the most, or just need to keep an eye on to ensure they get done what you want them to get done? This person is one of the biggest encouragers of you to micromanage, not just them, but everybody. If you can stop micromanaging them, then you stop that encouragement. Work more closely with them to train them and curb your need to be a "helicopter boss." If you can do this with them, you'll be able to do it with anybody on your team.

Getting to the heart

Patrick Lencioni in his Bestselling book *"The 5 Dysfunctions of a Team"* notes trust as the foundation of any great team. If that fundamental foundation isn't in place, there is little left to build upon.

The effects of a lack of trust go far and wide for leaders, but one of the results is often micromanagement as the leader does not trust their team to do the job effectively. If you want to handle trust issues in the workplace there is a simple remedy that works every time … communication.

Communication is the lifeblood of trust. If you communicate with your team more you will come to trust them more and vice versa. Why is that?

Better understanding – When you talk through issues you will discover things on both sides. As communication builds over time, you understand each other better. This makes all future communication more effective, and creates a positive feedback loop that leads to even better understanding and communication.

Reality check – It may be that the employee has a fear of failing on a particular task. If you're being open when discussing things, your own failures will pop up from time to time. This is very freeing for the employee to hear and helps you to curb any propensity you have for perfectionism. Both are essential for trust to be built.

More accessibility – If you have opened up the lines of communication then you are more accessible. The reason the "open door policy" was such a rage over the last couple of decades was it was supposed to assist in leader accessibility. However, communicating is a far more lasting and effective method of making you accessible in the ways you need.

One of the negative effects of micromanagement is it destroys the empowerment of the team. Basically they don't think you trust them to do their jobs. If you don't trust your team you can create a negative feedback loop where your team knows you don't trust them to handle the task and begins wondering why you don't. This leads to self-doubt and a slowdown in overall production.

"Your micro-management is actually a **method of procrastinating and avoiding** what you probably should be doing."

The myth of "busy"

It is often the case in organizations that it is better to be able to talk to your boss about 10 small things you are working on as opposed to three big things. The example I use to demonstrate the impact of this is that 10 pennies in my pocket may sound like a whole lot more money when they jingle around than three dimes do, but the three dimes are worth a whole lot more.

Leaders are often just as trained in this as their employees. When there is free time on their calendar they quickly go about the department looking for something they can review, something they can take over, or some place they can contribute in an effort to appear effective. The effect is usually the opposite as you've taken time away from more important things so you can hear that "jingle" of ten pennies in your pocket. To address this:

Know your role – This can be an issue with leaders who have risen through the ranks. It's very easy during busy times, in emergencies, or when you don't know what else to do, to roll up your sleeves and jump in to help. Remember your role is to ensure your team is able to function at maximum productivity. Usually the contribution you could personally make by jumping into the trenches pales in comparison to the support you could give them in other ways.

Don't interrupt your own workflow – Looking over your team's shoulders and asking for unnecessary updates interrupts your own workflow. One of the reasons micromanagers are so ineffective is they are jumping between so many small tasks and updates.

Be aware of the "attention to detail fallacy" – The problem with using "attention to detail" as a justification for your actions is it is never ending. There is always another detail just out of your reach; knowing exactly what is going on at exactly every moment in time and exactly what the next steps are and what effects those steps is a recipe for eventually focusing on things of close to zero importance.

Most leaders don't have the amount of time they would like to have to run their organizations. The problem is that just as many of them may fill what little time frees up with the wrong type of work ... and that can lead down the path to career and organizational failure.

OK, maybe it isn't all bad

After calling out the places and ways you need to stop micromanaging your team, it's time to talk about areas where you should be micromanaging. Or to use better terminology, "where you need to maintain firmer control."

Hiring – One of the most important areas that affect the long term health of the organization is who you allow to join your team. Given it is semi-infrequent and its importance, you should seek as much input as possible into who comes on board and how the process works for sourcing candidates, vetting candidates, and making the final decision.

Change – When you are instituting change there are a number of dependencies, problems, variables, and opportunities that arise. For that reason, it is a good idea to be deeply involved in any sort of change within your organization so you can give it the greatest chance for success.

Problems – When problems arise either financially or operationally, this is where your team looks to you for the solution. Yes, you want to empower your team to fix issues themselves, but you need to first lead the way. You also want to be involved after the fact to do the root-cause analysis.

High-risk and high profile issues – Based on the profile or risk involved (either from a liability, financial, or P.R. perspective) it would be wise to be deeply involved as you are likely to be asked for updates from your boss or even higher up the corporate ladder.

It's important you acknowledge these areas, but not seek them out as an excuse to fall back into bad habits. What is consistent in all of these is they are high priority items based on their nature. For this reason, they aren't truly "micro" management.

EXPRESSWAY

Start with your best people – If you're having problems stopping your micromanaging tendencies, then why not focus on not micromanaging your best people. After all, they should have the best chance of "flying on their own wings." If you can step away from them a little bit, and the world doesn't come crashing down, then you build some positive momentum in addressing everyone else.

Dealing with your micromanaging boss

Your team isn't alone; you have a boss too. And just like you, your boss may struggle from time to time with micromanagement. So how do you deal with your boss's micromanagement? You employ some of the same techniques you employed when dealing with your own micromanagement.

Updates – Instead of having them pop over to your cube or office at random times looking for updates, or hovering over you while commenting on the work, why don't you offer to update them? This shows some accountability over your work, but what you're really looking for is some uninterrupted time where you can get the work done. Maybe it's offering to update them on progress in an hour, tomorrow, or sometime next week, but this helps put the control in your hands.

As you continue to update them on project after project and start building trust, you want to start trying to stretch out the time between updates so you cut down the interruptions even further.

Second steps – Lots of people shoot themselves in the foot with a micromanaging boss because they don't ask for clarification, or ask questions in general. When they give you one step in the process and you're clear on it, ask for clarification on the next step. Again, we're looking to cut down the number of times you interact with them over the course of the project. Also, when they are more assured they've explained themselves better, they'll be more apt to trust you with the task.

Examples – If they won't volunteer examples of what the finished product looks like, or examples of steps along the way, then by all means ask for them. The more information you have, the better your chance of meeting their expectations.

Touting your contribution – Another way to build trust is to tout your expertize and success once you have a track record. This can make them reassess their concern over how you will handle the things they assign you. Now this doesn't mean bragging, this means calling out the successes in more subtle ways when you turn things in, or as a reminder when they might be considering walking down the road of micromanagement.

Being able to manage not only your own micromanagement, but the micromanagement of your boss as well can have an enormous impact on the productivity of your team and yourself. And it just makes for a better work environment in general.

You Know the Route, Now Start Driving

What one tactic from the "Better" or "Great" will you employ now that you are done with the chapter?

What actions will you take to improve?

What date and time will you take action?

When will you review the results?

What is one other tactic you wish to employ when you are satisfied with the results of the first?

Souvenirs From The Trip

How to Be Better

Are you on schedule?
Two techniques that will make you feel better about giving up some control.

Hitting the learning curve(ball)
Three things that will assist you and your employee while they learn.

"What" not "How"
The technique that eliminates most micromanagement.

No touching the "finishing touches"
Why you shouldn't jump into the process right at the finish line.

Reminisce about your last vacation
Your wake-up call to the effect of micromanaging your employees.

A Pothole to Avoid
One of the worst, yet most tempting, places to micromanage.

How to Be Great

Stop playing dodgeball with performance
What your micromanagement is often addressing.

Getting to the heart
Three techniques to foster more trust.

The myth of "busy"
How to be busy with more important things.

OK, maybe it isn't all bad
Four areas you still need to be incredibly involved in.

Dealing with your micromanaging boss
The four things you can do to disuade your boss from micromanaging you.

"Expressways"
Examples
You don't need to be guiding them if they have a guide in front of them.

Start with your best people
Where to focus if you're having problems eliminating micromanagement from your leadership.

6.

Dealing with Failure

Your inevitable opportunity

FAILURE IS SO POWERFUL IN YOUR CAREER BECAUSE IT **FORCES YOU TO TAKE ACTION,** AND TESTS THAT ACTION WITH **THE RESULTS YOU ACHIEVE**

Are You Heading Down a Dead End?

Do "unusual" and "unique" situations happen frequently around your mistakes and failures?

Is there a lot of blaming taking place in your department?

Are you hearing about failures long after they take place?

Has there been nothing new or innovative done in your area recently?

Are mistakes being repeated?

Sorry, It's Inevitable

There is an old quote from Aristotle that states, "There is only one way to avoid criticism: do nothing, say nothing, and be nothing." And I believe the same applies to failure. Failure is a part of leadership, just like it is a part of life. It's how many people force themselves to learn, through the pain and embarrassment of making a mistake and coming up short of the goal.

When you fail, it puts you in the spotlight. You can make the most of that opportunity by quickly, calmly and professionally addressing the failure. Or you can fumble around and make yourself look worse. How you deal with failure will determine, more than almost anything else, how successful you are in your career.

When you fail, your boss, peers, and employees will be watching you closely and asking themselves these questions:

Am I dealing with someone who:

- Is completely truthful or tries to create confusion to cover up the issue?
- Accepts responsibility, or looks for an excuse or someone to blame?
- Learns from mistakes, or repeats them over and over again?

Handle failure well, and you will shine through these questions and be on your way to making failure something that launches you forward instead of holding you back.

Why Leaders Take a Wrong Turn

Make the pain go away quickly

Many leaders choose to not learn from their failures and mistakes simply because they don't want to spend any time dwelling on them. Failure isn't fun, but you know what is even less fun than making a mistake? Picking apart every aspect of what went into the failure to ensure you learn from it. That can be excruciating, and is why many leaders choose to avoid it.

They spend energy hiding it

Whether they don't want their boss or team to know, or because they don't want to do the work to fix it, leaders may choose to hide the failure from everyone while they work on fixing it in the background. This delaying of the inevitable avoids the learning they can get from their failure, increases the risk of it having a negative impact on their career, and almost always reduces overall productivity.

The leader justifies failure

"Weeeeell, it really isn't that bad" is a cop-out. And trying to defend the reasons it isn't that bad in the first place is wasted time on the leader's part that could be spent on something productive. Minimizing the impact of a mistake minimizes the impact of the resolution, minimizes the learning, and magnifies the chances it occurs again.

Over-reacting

Many leaders actually move too quickly for their own good when faced with a failure. They will assume the worst, go into panic mode, and quickly reach out to as many people as possible to help them. What this does is give them a lot of attention and a lot of resources. While the mistake or failure may get dealt with under this scenario, this isn't dealing with a failure in the right way from an overall organizational perspective.

The issue is the leader did not carefully assess the situation and marshal resources to deal with it and learn from it. Instead, they chose the "nuclear option" of throwing all of the resources they could gather at it. This isn't leading thoughtfully, it's leading carelessly, and it results in the leader not truly learning and developing from their failure.

How to Be Better

Recognize it

The first step in dealing with failures is to see them in the first place. Many people gloss over this part because they think mistakes just jump up in the middle of the day with a big flashing sign on them. Some of them do, but especially when we start talking about management and leadership of people, they can be subtler and more difficult to spot.

Most of the reasons listed in the "Wrong Turn" section get at this tendency to avoid, deflect, and ignore whenever possible. You have a lot on your plate and recognizing failures does nothing but add to that work. The concept you need to get familiar with is the quicker you recognize, acknowledge, and get to work on a mistake, the quicker you will get past it. Which brings up the biggest opportunity in recognizing failures:

Failures in process are not final

Being able to recognize the signs of a potential failure, before it becomes a failure is one of the things that separates great leaders from mediocre ones. What do I mean by recognizing signs?

- Recognizing sales aren't as strong in the first month of the quarter as they need to be to reach the quarterly goal
- Recognizing Robert is struggling to learn the new process
- Recognizing an increase in complaints

Now you might just hope that these things turn themselves around by themselves, and wait to address them until they become an emergency. But all of the signs above are harbingers of eventual failure. Recognizing them as such, and acting on them is how you limit your failures.

ROAD WORK AHEAD

Right now, as you're reading this, there is a failure in process you have placed as a low priority, are hoping turns around, or are just plain avoiding. But what if it doesn't turn around? Will you be able to avoid it then? Find a failure in process in your department you aren't addressing and set about addressing it immediately. Recognizing a problem before it becomes a crisis is a hallmark of great leadership.

"Do you know who admits to failures freely, gracefully and with thought on the resolution? Great leaders, that's who."

Fessing up to failure

For most of us, the most painful part of failing is admitting it to others. This embarrassment is the root cause of many dodges and delays, but as we've said already, failures and mistakes are inevitable in your work and in the work of those around you, so take some solace in the fact that whomever you are reporting it to has found themselves in the same situation. Consider the following when reporting a mistake or failure:

- Report your failures as quickly as possible so your boss doesn't find out about them from someone else.
- Apologize without assigning blame and without sounding defensive.
- Have a plan ready and do whatever you can to correct your mistake as quickly as you can.
- Show you thought about what led to the failure.
- Commit to not making that mistake again and explain how you will avoid it.

Do you know who admits to failures freely, gracefully and with thought on the resolution? Great leaders, that's who. The quicker you acknowledge responsibility, the quicker it all gets solved. And if you follow the list above, you may just have turned a failure into something that demonstrates the kind of leadership others want to see.

The quick and the careless

When fixing a failure, make sure you aren't setting yourself up for another. You have put yourself in the spotlight, so it pays to move quickly, but at the same time carefully. Too many leaders rush to make up for their failure, stumble and make mistakes along the way that cause even more problems. It makes sense to "measure twice and cut once." One of the best ways to do that is to open up communication with peers and employees as you put together and execute the plan. Having another set of eyes to look at things creates a natural double-check that doesn't slow the process down. Fix the mistake quickly, but ensure it is fixed.

"Booby Trap" future mistakes

The typical way leaders choose to prevent mistakes is to come up with a procedural fix. This can be a new procedure, or it can be an add-on to existing procedures. In many cases, there isn't a better way to address it, but this is actually the least preferred way of preventing mistakes because it adds work to your team, slows down the overall process, and tends to turn people into robots. This often occurs when a mistake is particularly painful and you end up "managing the exception," which means addressing the once in a thousand mistake with a process that gets instituted each and every time.

What I prefer to look at are "triggers" or "booby traps" that will alert you to an issue before it becomes a failure:

Metrics – Like a pressure gauge that has a red zone, some metrics can be used to indicate an issue is brewing. Things like, conversion rates going down, store traffic declining, backorders building, production slowing can all indicate to you there may be a problem on the horizon. If you can back these up with procedures once something occurs, you limit the impact on the operation to just those times when it is absolutely necessary to address.

Event triggers – Similar to the above, when an event occurs like a spike in orders, a certain number of people calling out sick, or a delay in shipping, you take action. This can include heightened awareness, calling in more people, adjusting process flow, etc. The key in both of these instances is you have a procedure in place, but only apply it to the instances when it is necessary, not all instances.

These "triggers" can accomplish exactly what you want to accomplish without burdening the operation with constant double-checks, checklists, and procedures.

EXPRESSWAY

The learning you're missing most – Most of us know we are supposed to learn from failure, but this ignores another huge source of learning; from your successes. You succeed far more than you fail, and your success teaches you just as much: What works, what should be repeated, where your strengths are, what information is valuable, etc. So don't just focus on learning from failure, learn from your successes as well.

Look in the rearview mirror

Making mistakes and failing is hard, and it can send you down a depressing road when it happens. This negativity doesn't help you get through the work of correcting and learning, it can often prevent it. But past success can create a defense against this negativity and can actually point the way out in some cases.

You likely do a terrible job of giving yourself credit for your successes. Part of it is you are always on the lookout for problems that need to be fixed, so you aren't looking for success. The other issue is you generally expect to be successful, so it isn't particularly remarkable when success happens. After all, why would you start something if you didn't expect to be successful at it?

Of course, the funny or sad thing is your successes vastly outnumber your failures. If you find yourself with a lack of confidence in any way, there is a ready supply of examples from recent and past history that support the idea you should be confident, and at the same time, shouldn't be concerned about failure. Leveraging your prior successes is an easy way to give you confidence to push past failure.

A Pothole to Avoid

Decisions that are made out of fear are almost always bad decisions. Part of dealing with failure is dealing with the fear of failure. You can't allow yourself to be ruled by what could go wrong, you need to strike a balance with what could go right as well. When you find yourself facing more fear in your decisions, work on being more thoughtful, and less emotional. One of the best ways to do that is to lean on all of the lessons in this chapter. When you prepare, you can move more confidently through your decisions.

How to Be Great

Cut it out at the root

Once you're past the initial trauma, it's a good time to do a deep dive into the failure to ensure you have learned all you can. If you haven't been able to get crystal clear on the below questions to really get to the cause of the failure they can help you gather an immense amount of information to work with to learn and prevent the failure from occurring again:

1) What was the sequence of events that led to the failure?
2) Were there any bad assumptions made?
3) What would you do differently if this exact situation happened again?
4) Was there information you know now that would have been useful in preventing the failure?
5) How can you avoid this in the future?

The information gathered from these questions helps you put on paper the things you can learn from and help move your next steps and solutions forward with greater insight.

ROAD WORK AHEAD

You can do this exercise at any time. Take your last failure. It might have been yesterday or last month, and run it through these questions. I'll be willing to bet you learn at least one thing you hadn't considered before.

"SUCCESS IS NOT FINAL, FAILURE IS NOT FATAL:

IT IS THE COURAGE TO CONTINUE THAT COUNTS."

~Winston Churchill

Have you put failure on repeat?

Repeated failures are indicative of not putting forth the effort to be successful. It's a simple and hard truth. An example many leaders can relate to is allowing poor performance by an employee to continue because you are exhausted of coming up with new ideas to address it. When most leaders would give up, you need to challenge yourself to lean in instead.

If there is a repeated failure, then you need to challenge your assumptions. You're seeing something wrong, or not seeing the whole picture. Go back to the questions in the prior section and re-answer them. Allowing a failure to repeat, no matter how small, opens the door for further failure by either your team or yourself. The first time it may have been a mistake, the second time it is more likely to be a choice.

Partner up

If you failed, it makes sense to get an outside opinion. In almost every case of failure, somebody on the team saw warning signs. It may be embarrassing, but often you can't see your own blind spots and an outside observer has insight that can help you.

Asking somebody what else they saw and how they might handle the situation helps give you new ideas, new feedback, and a partner to help with the issue moving forward.

Don't treat mistakes like they are crimes

If you doubt that failure is often the source of opportunity, look at this list of 15 ways to harness the mistakes you make for your benefit.

- Speed change in yourself and others
- Serve as a warning
- Point you to something you did not know
- Suggest new options you had not considered

- Tell you something about your skill level
- Help you recognize changing circumstances
- Show you what works and what doesn't work
- Encourage you to want to work better
- Teach you the value of forgiveness
- Teach you how to experiment
- Make you more humble
- Can highlight failures of judgments
- Show you when you are not listening
- Slow you down when you need to
- Reveal your blind spots

EXPRESSWAY

The least painful way to learn – If you don't want to learn through failing, then just look around. There are failures being made all around you from peers, bosses, competitors, and employees. Just because you didn't make the failure, doesn't mean you can't look into it and see what you can learn. It's a whole lot quicker and easier than waiting until you make mistakes yourself.

Sharing is caring

Do you want to hold yourself accountable for learning from failure? Commit to sharing what you learned with your team. Not only does this help you, it also helps your team learn from your failures, lest they make their own.

Creating an environment where failure is accepted (as long as it isn't careless, and is learned from) is a hallmark of a healthy and innovative organization. If you as the leader set the tone by not only admitting your failures, but talking about the lessons learned, then your team will be more apt to follow suit.

Forget it

Once you have learned from a mistake and prevented it from occurring again, it ceases to be of use. In fact, it can become a hindrance to your success as it slows you down and in some cases can prevent you from moving forward.

The importance of learning from your mistakes completely and implementing preventative measures along with the fix for the mistake is it frees you to move on. If there is nothing left to learn or implement, then the mistake is of no current or future value.

You Know the Route, Now Start Driving

What one tactic from the "Better" or "Great" will you employ now that you are done with the chapter?

What actions will you take to improve?

What date and time will you take action?

When will you review the results?

What is one other tactic you wish to employ when you are satisfied with the results of the first?

Souvenirs From The Trip

How to Be Better
Recognize it
Failure is often subtle, and there is one type of failure it pays to recognize early.

Fessing up to failure
Five steps to take when you need to admit to failure.

The quick and the careless
The communication you should have to ensure your "fix" doesn't create another failure.

"Booby Trap" future mistakes
Two methods that will help you identify failure before it occurs.

Look in the rearview mirror
The area you don't focus on enough.

A Pothole to Avoid
How fear can create even more failure.

How to Be Great
Cut it out at the root
Five questions you can ask to get to the root cause of the failure and how to prevent it.

Have you put that failure on repeat?
What you need to do if you find yourself repeating your failures.

Partner up

The value in acknowledging the perceptions of others.

Don't treat mistakes like they are crimes

15 good things that come out of failure.

Sharing is caring

The step that holds you accountable for learning from failure.

Forget it

Things that are of no use need to be discarded.

"Expressways"

The learning you're missing most

Failure isn't the only source of learning.

The least painful way to learn

You don't need to be the only one failing in order to learn.

7.

Hiring

The most lasting decision

THE THREE P'S OF HIRING GREAT PEOPLE: PREPARATION, PRACTICE AND PATIENCE.

Are You Heading Down a Dead End?

Have you ever asked, "Remind me again... why did we hire that guy?"

Do you assess whether a candidate is an organizational or cultural fit for you?

Do you do most of the talking when you interview?

Do you have a scoring mechanism for candidates?

Do you have any means of questioning or checking if what they say on their resume is true?

Panning For Gold

Hiring should be fun. It's like picking teams in Elementary School where you have the first pick of anybody to be on your team. It's an opportunity to make your life instantly easier at work as long as you make the right choice, and it will be your legacy for the organization.

But most leaders look at the hiring process with a sense of dread. The reason? It is a huge layout of time and effort they haven't accounted for and therefore will be forced to squeeze in. Couple that with the fact most leaders don't get enough practice doing it and you're in a situation ripe for being rushed and ineffective. Yes, every leader knows how important it is to hire the right people, but most get frustrated when the right person doesn't just fall in their lap.

I'll come right out and say there isn't a process to make hiring quick and still make it effective, but there are some basics you can cover so you're getting the most out of it, are comfortable doing it, and have the absolute best chance to find an amazing addition to your staff.

Why Leaders Take a Wrong Turn

Don't have time to do it right

All leaders are busy and find their days packed with things to do, so it's no wonder they rush through the hiring process when faced with four hours' worth of interviews in one afternoon. Couple this with a need to have the person start right away, and you have a rush, rush, rush attitude which sets an environment that doesn't guard against mistakes.

ROAD WORK AHEAD

One of the best things you can do is to reframe your perspective so you aren't rushing. Instead of thinking somebody is going to start in three weeks, because that's what you really need, think of it as if someone is going to start in three months. While that may sound like a lot of time, when you consider how long it will take to source applicants, conduct interviews, have them give notice at their current employer, train them, and for that person to become proficient at the job, then three months is reasonable. When you consider an amazing candidate won't take as long to train and be proficient, you actually have incentive to be patient. If you want the best for your team, you need to prepare yourself to be choosy.

Don't plan for it

The first problem leaders run into is they don't have plans for what to do if they need to fill a spot in their organization. They haven't identified people who can be promoted, they don't have a candidate pool of new-hires available, they don't know what questions to ask in interviews, and they don't have a plan for "on-boarding" a new-hire into the organization. They start from scratch every time. So when the "surprise" hits and they need to hire someone, they have no way of getting a head start on filling the position.

Were never shown how

Considering the importance of hiring the right people, it's shocking how little (if any) training is done on how to go about the process in a way that ensures you get the right person on board.

Sure, every leader has been through interviews before, and there may be some forms to fill out that HR provides, but really, is that it? In this case it isn't the leader's fault they don't hire right, it's the organization's fault. And unless the leader takes it upon themselves to educate themselves, they are left guessing what they should and shouldn't do far more than they should be.

How to Be Better

Do you know what "amazing" looks like?

If you don't have a specific goal, then success is far less likely. This goes for hiring just as much as it does anything else. One of the best things you can do when hiring is to spend time finding out exactly what you are looking for:

- What traits and skills do your most successful employees share?
- What traits and skills would you like to add to your team?
- What attitude do you want, and what would someone demonstrate who had the attitude?

Simply getting clear on what you are looking for, putting it on paper, and reviewing it before every interview will significantly increase your likelihood of finding an amazing candidate, and avoiding a terrible one.

Becoming a salesman

Great candidates are picky and demanding, and if you want to hire them you will need to market yourself and your organization or they may never even apply.

What you need to understand is you are in a fight for great talent with other organizations, just as much as you are for customers. To that end, you need to put your "best foot forward" just as much as you are expecting your applicants to do so themselves. Here are some ways to start:

What does your team like about their job? – A great background check for you as you start this process is to simply ask your team what they like about the job. This information lets you know what the potential candidate can look forward to and what should be highlighted in the job description and during the interview.

Can you tweak the job title? – The first thing an applicant sees is the job title. Just like any advertising, the first impression is of extra importance. Titles like "Customer Support Representative" and "Sales Clerk" are disasters waiting to happen to your time and sanity when looking over applicants. Sometimes a simple word change like "Coordinator" instead of "Clerk" or "Rep" can make all of the difference. Changes like "Success" instead of "Service" can also work, but be careful to match your corporate culture. Whatever you can do to make the job title more interesting and appealing can make a big difference in who is interested. Just ask yourself whether the title is something you would want on your resume.

Are the responsibilities challenging? – This is where you can review those areas your employees like, and make sure they are included in the job description you post. Great employees will want to grow and add to their skillsets, so it is important to highlight the empowerment areas they have and all of the technical skills they will develop. You want candidates to go "Wow!" when they read how much the position is responsible for. This attracts great candidates and scares off the weaker ones.

Is the pay competitive? – Kip Tindell is the CEO of The Container Store, one of the perennial companies listed on "Best Workplaces" lists. He explains his high pay for line level employees thusly, "One employee with passion is worth three average employees." If the pay is competitive, then great! But if it isn't then you'll need to address it one way or the other. While you may have no say over the pay rate of the position (most leaders don't), if you find it isn't competitive, then you know you will need to address other areas of attractiveness like job description, flexible work arrangements, benefits, etc.

Creating a great job posting is as much a marketing effort as anything else and can either be something that attracts amazing candidates, or encourages them to look elsewhere.

The basics you were never taught

Many leaders have next to no experience interviewing from the employer's side of the desk. Luckily there are just a few things you can keep in mind that will have a significant impact on the value you get out of the interview:

Preparation – The other reason you want to know what an "amazing" employee looks like is so you can ask questions about those traits and skills; "Tell me about a time you demonstrated _____", "What kind of experience do you have with _____?" You should have 5-10 standard questions you ask every applicant written down ahead of time for your notes.

Go through their resume in the 5-10 minutes before the interview and note areas you want to hear more about. This should be limited to no more than 10 to keep the interview on track. This is an opportunity to drill down into their experience.

Describe the position and company up front – This helps you "speak the same language" over the course of the interview, and allows the candidate to self-address areas that apply to the job instead of going off on tangents that don't apply.

Don't ask yes/no questions – You want to give them an opportunity to elaborate whenever possible. Start questions with What, How, or Why and you'll be fine.

Don't talk too much – The candidate should be doing at least 80% of the talking during the time between introductions and when you ask them if they have questions. FYI, that's 24 minutes of a 30-minute interview.

Don't take a "walk" through the resume – You have the resume right in front of you. What do you need to know? Ask it. Don't hand over control of the interview.

Leave time for questions – While you may be able to cover many questions when introducing the positon and organization, an amazing applicant should still have a few to ask. It's courteous and often enlightening to give them a chance to ask.

There are many more aspects to interviewing, but these address some of the most common shortfalls in how leaders conduct them. If you can get these right, you'll be ahead of most interviewers out there.

The age old hiring debate

Some of the worst interviews you conduct will be with the most experienced candidates. The reason is they know they have the experience and they feel entitled to the position. In these cases, it's no wonder they have 10 years of experience in the same position, because they don't have the attitude for a promotion.

Skills will prove useless if there isn't the right attitude to go with them. For this reason, you need to structure questions that delve into the attitude traits you have identified. You can teach anybody a skill given enough time, but it is almost impossible to correct an attitude issue.

"The secret of my success is that we have gone to exceptional lengths to hire the best people in the world."

~Steve Jobs

You're being judged

Amazing candidates are very similar to interviewers in that they have choices. They have choices of where they can go, and they are selective in choosing the right fit for their career. They won't just go anywhere that offers them a job. Have you ever been to an interview that started late? In a messy office? Where it didn't seem like the interviewer had read your resume or prepared any questions? Did it leave you with a good impression? That impression can cause you to lose great people. Consider the following to ensure you make a great impression:

On time – You expect them to be there early; the courteous thing is to bring them in on time. This often means you can't go as back-to back with the interviews as you want, but I'm sure there is something that needs your attention in the time spaces between.

Look the part – Dress codes vary wildly in today's work environment, but the rule of thumb is to dress like you're attending an important meeting (because you are).

Be engaged – Look them in the eye, take notes, smile, lean in, nod your head, and otherwise be interested in what they are saying. If you aren't interested in what they are saying now, then you leave the impression you won't be interested in what they say if they are hired.

Be organized – Have their resume in front of you, clean up your office a little, have your questions prepared, know where they are sitting, know where you are sitting, and maintain control of the interview.

Finish strong – Ask if they have any questions you could answer and let them know what to expect as far as next steps are concerned.

If you fail in these areas the candidate may rightfully wonder, "If you aren't willing to handle hiring, with professionalism and attention, what other important things do you treat this way?"

A Pothole to Avoid

Many leaders face the hiring process alone, which is a mistake on a couple of different levels. You have resources all around you, and in this important area, you need to make sure you are utilizing them. If you haven't interviewed many people before, ask someone in your organization with a lot of interviewing experience to help you and sit in on the interviews with you. There is nothing like having a coach in the room with you to speed your learning curve. The second reason to bring someone else into the process is to get a second opinion. You are human, and you will miss things and over focus on things. A second person, either in the room with you, or who can conduct a second interview is invaluable. There's no reason that a team leader or supervisor can't interview a candidate. Even line level employees have an opinion and perspective you don't that can assist you. So don't go through the hiring process alone. You'll find it easier, and your decisions better if you don't.

How to Be Great

Interviewing 201

Now that you have some of the basics down for interviewing, let's step into some of the more in depth concepts:

Interview potential, not past – What they did in the past is great, but it isn't what you are looking for. You want an idea of what they can do, what they are capable of, and just how high they can climb within your organization. Hiring for the specific job opening is fine, but it's always nice to bring someone in who you believe is capable of growing into increasing responsibility in the organization.

Probe for mis-truths – People lie on resumes and in interviews. Most are white lies, but many aren't. That's why it's important to ask clarifying questions on those things that are most important to you. You don't need to be paranoid, but you do need to be vigilant and do your due diligence.

"Did" not "would" – It's always preferable to hear about a situation that "did" take place as opposed to "would" take place. While you don't want to discredit the candidate if they don't have specific experience, one should certainly be weighted over the other.

Be curious about lateral moves – If a candidate is applying for a lateral move, it's important they answer the question of "why" they want to move. What you want to be wary of are those candidates who are regularly dissatisfied with their jobs and employers. There are perfectly acceptable reasons for moving laterally between organizations, but you want to hear it from them.

ROAD WORK AHEAD

If you want to get better at interviewing and hiring, then you need to practice. While you certainly have plenty of things to do, taking a few extra candidates who appear marginal so you can get some more experience is a great idea. There is a chance an amazing candidate exists at the "fringes," and it gives you extra practice. If you haven't conducted at least 50 interviews, you are a novice (and many would argue you would need over 100), so any opportunity you have to practice should be sought out.

What do the judges' scorecards say?

When deciding on what candidate to select, do you always have a crystal clear understanding of why you chose one over the other? Most leaders don't. You have the 5-10 questions you created that address the most important traits and skills a successful employee needs to have, why not take those questions to the next level and score the answers?

It can be as simple as a 1 to 5 scale based on how you liked their answer, but it's important to decide ahead of time what is worthy of a "5" versus a "3". In these cases, get clearer on the behaviors surrounding these traits.

For instance, if you have a question on managing in a crisis, a score of "3" may require that they evaluated before acting, whereas a "4" may require that they evaluated before acting and also listened to others.

Setting this up before the interview makes the interview less subjective and more focused on exactly what you need to get out of it.

A buffet of great candidates?

There will be times when you find more than one candidate who qualifies as "amazing," or one who you think would be a great fit for another opening in the organization. Amazing employees are rare, and you don't want to lose the opportunity to bring them on board, but if you don't have the ability to, consider the following:

Queue them – You may not have a position now, but make sure they know you are sincerely interested and ask them if they would be interested if a position opened up in the future? You might be surprised just how many of these candidates are indeed interested 3, 6, and 9 months later.

Do a friend a favor – If you have a sister department looking for people, and you think they might be a fit, recommend them to the position. If you can't bring them on board in your area, you can at least bring them into the organization.

"Skills will prove useless if there isn't **the right attitude to go with them.**"

Culture club

Ensuring the candidate is going to fit into your organizational culture is an important step many leaders don't take. An amazing candidate won't be amazing if they aren't put in an environment where they can thrive. One of the reasons people don't hire for cultural fit is they think it is difficult to determine whether someone will be a fit through an interview. It is actually much easier than you think.

If you want to know the behaviors and traits of employees who fit your culture:

Just look at your existing staff, identify who emulates the culture best, and identify their behaviors and traits.

The next thing to do is determining interview questions that help understand what sort of culture the applicant likes and works best in. You need to be able to answer the following three questions for yourself before the interview is over:

- Do their values match ours?
- Will their style of work match the way we do things here?
- Is the work going to be meaningful to them?

How you find out the answers is by asking the right questions in the interview. I've included some examples of questions you could ask, but depending on your culture you will want to tweak, add, and/or delete to serve your specific needs.

- Which of our values resonates with you the most?
- What kind of work environment do you prefer?
- What kind of values are important to you?
- In what way would you say the role you are applying for is meaningful?
- What is an example from your work experience that you feel reinforced one of our values?

- In what ways do you think you are a fit with our culture?
- How would you describe our culture, based on what you have seen and heard so far?
- Are you comfortable with our values and what they mean?

Being a good culture fit is as important as attitude and experience, so treat it as such by making it a part of your interviews.

EXPRESSWAY

Always be looking for talent – Really amazing employees are scarce, and you should be looking for them even if you don't have an opening. Whether it is industry events, conferences, or simply asking your colleagues and friends, there's no reason you can't interview somebody even when you don't have an opening (as long as they are aware of that). The timing may not work out when openings occur, but when it does, it makes hiring so much smoother.

Hiring isn't the last step

Your hiring job isn't over once a great candidate has accepted the job. There is still one essential step that is routinely overlooked and can have a detrimental impact on you being able to keep that great employee, as well as you being able to get the maximum productivity out of them; Onboarding the new hire in the best way possible. If you miss this step you risk undoing all of your hard work up until this point.

If you've been working long enough you will no doubt have come across a scenario where someone (perhaps you) shows up for their first day and the process is disorganized, poorly thought out, or completely different than what you were told in the interview. In many cases this drops the great candidate's expectations of performance they will be held to and in the worst cases, encourages them to leave.

The Human Capitalist conducted a survey and found that 22 percent of turnover takes place within the initial 45 days and 16 percent in the course of the first week. And it isn't poor performers washing out; it's some of the best prospects who cut their losses. Remember, great candidates have options and goals. If they aren't being served by you beyond just a paycheck, they'll quickly look elsewhere.

It doesn't need to take more than an hour of coordination to put together a plan and schedule for bringing a new hire on board that makes the right impression, gets them excited to use their talent, and smooths the path to integrating them into the operation. Below are five things you should be prepared to address in your onboarding to make it successful:

Have a schedule – It immediately lets them know you are thoughtful and methodical in your approach to leadership and you will be providing them clear direction so they can prepare to excel.

Introductions – Whether it is taking them on a tour, or scheduling departments and executives to come in and speak with them, in today's collaborative workplaces, the quicker you introduce everyone the better. This is a great supplement to their schedule in helping to give them a "map" of the organization.

One thing vitally important to amazing candidates is exposure to executives. This is a fantastic time to reinforce how important the new hires are to the organization and reinforce the message and goals of the organization by having executives come by and speak to them.

Give them a "go-to" person – You may be heading up the training and onboarding process, but it is important to give them a mentor from amongst the team right away. This accomplishes a few things: it helps introduce them to one person they will be working alongside on a regular basis which will make them more comfortable, it gives them someone else to answer basic questions they might not be inclined to bother you with, and it shows them you develop your employees (hence the position of "mentor").

Give them "real world" work on the first day – One of the best things you can do when onboarding is to give them exposure to their duties right away. This shows you expect action in their day to day work and for them to move forward when they are uncomfortable. It can be a small task or duty you personally train them on, and see they are supervised while doing it on their own. The bottom line: get them into the "real world" mix immediately.

One-on-ones – Possibly the most important thing for you to do throughout the onboarding process is to have your first one-on-one meeting with the new-hire. This gives you a chance to reinforce why you hired them, the importance of their role, and what your expectations are. But most importantly, it's time for you to set goals with them. The most common timeframe is 90 day goals since that is a period of time where they should be comfortable in their role. This meeting also gives you an opportunity to get feedback on the training and onboarding process so you can continually improve it.

If you address these areas, you have given your newly hired employees their best chance to thrive.

You Know the Route, Now Start Driving

What one tactic from the "Better" or "Great" will you employ now that you are done with the chapter?

What actions will you take to improve?

What date and time will you take action?

When will you review the results?

What is one other tactic you wish to employ when you are satisfied with the results of the first?

Souvenirs From The Trip

How to Be Better
Do you know what "amazing" looks like?
How to find out exactly what you are looking for.

Becoming a salesman
Four questions you need to answer to be able to attract amazing talent.

The basics you were never taught
Six interviewing concepts most leaders miss, but which have a huge impact on what you get out of an interview.

The age old hiring debate
Why experience fails many job applicants.

You're being judged
Five things candidates judge you on.

A Pothole to Avoid
Why you shouldn't go through the hiring process alone.

How to Be Great
Interviewing 201
Four "next level" tips for conducting a great interview.

What do the judges' scorecards say?
How to make an interview less subjective.

A buffet of great candidates?

Two things you can do when you find more great candidates than you have positions for.

Culture club

The questions required to hire the right fit for your organizational culture.

Hiring isn't the last step

Why what you do after hiring someone is just as important as hiring them in the first place.

"Expressways"

Repel the bad applicants

The technique that will help save you the time of handling unqualified candidates.

Always be looking for talent

Why you should be in "hiring mode" all of the time.

8.

Team Building

Making 1+1 = 3

TEAM BUILDING ISN'T ABOUT **GIMMICKY ACTIVITIES.** IT IS ABOUT FOSTERING AN ENVIRONMENT WHERE **UNDERSTANDING AND COLLABORATION THRIVE.**

Are You Heading Down a Dead End?

Are there a lot of misunderstandings among employees?

Is there a lot of blame being spread amongst the team?

Does fairness come up routinely when employees complain?

Does the department have attendance issues?

Do people rarely help each other finish tasks or projects?

Is there bickering or arguments occurring regularly?

More Useful Than Duct Tape

Teamwork is amazing in an organizational setting. It can cover up weakness. Make up for strategic mistakes. It improves morale. It encourages and motivates. And it speeds up communication. No wonder it is universally recognized as one of the things every leader should strive to instill in their team.

But how exactly do you do it? That is the question that leaves most leaders struggling and fumbling with activities, exercises, and tactics that are of marginal benefit and can border on the silly.

Building a great team goes much deeper than the standard team building exercises you may be familiar with (though they do have a place). When leaders focus on the foundational elements and the environment their teams work in, and getting those right, then teamwork can flourish. It isn't gimmicky, but it also isn't complicated.

One of the secrets of all of those team building exercises, and your team building efforts going forward, is it is very difficult for them to fail. The reason: employees understand the benefits of teamwork as well. So if an activity succeeds, it succeeds, but if it fails, the team will make the most out of it and will often have a shared experience that itself creates a closer team.

Why Leaders Take a Wrong Turn

Don't know how

While all leaders know teamwork and collaboration are things they should be striving for, often the standard routes to getting there seem a little ... well, silly. Trust falls, sack races, and exercises with blindfolds seem more appropriate for a high school summer camp than an organization. As much as teamwork gets talked about in organizations, there still isn't as much clarity on how to foster it.

Hire their mirror image

Diversity is one of the keys to great teams. A mix of different backgrounds and skills brought together is the recipe for accentuating strengths and minimizing weaknesses. Where leaders fail in setting up an environment for teamwork to thrive is when they hire people with similar backgrounds and interests as them. While this is great for rapport, it limits the heights the entire group can strive for.

Make the workplace competitive individually

One of the ways leaders motivate their teams is through competition. In many cases this means individual competition. When this technique is set up wrong, relied upon too often, or given too much importance in things like pay and benefits it can undermine all team building efforts as everyone is encouraged by the organization to fend for themselves.

Not clear on expectations and roles

Teamwork requires clear expectations and a clear definition of roles. Many leaders fail at teamwork because they have never set the foundation for what it is built upon. If an employee doesn't understand the role of the person sitting next to them, then it makes volunteering their help, or asking for help all the more difficult. If the same employee isn't clear on what they are expected to do, then they won't even know when to ask for assistance.

How to Be Better
* *

Why are you playing the game?

One of the reasons goal-setting is so successful in organizations is actually something on the periphery. It isn't the focus and planning on the goal itself, it is the aligning of everyone on the team behind a single effort. Instead of working on their own individual things in a vacuum, they see where their efforts fit in which gives them a greater sense of purpose. It gives them a common language with others on the team and helps everyone set priorities. If you are serious about fostering more teamwork, you need to determine a common goal all employees can work towards.

You want something that is affected by every member of your team and by every task they complete. It may take a little creative thinking and going through many layers and steps, but every job and tasks relate to the well-being of the organization in some way. In sporting events it is to score more points than the other team. This is accomplished by limiting how much the other team scores (defense), and scoring points yourself (offense). Each individual's efforts align to achieve that goal. Common goals that may relate to your area could be customer satisfaction, sales, production, shipping quotas or profitability.

Once you have a common goal set for your team, you can take it one step further and use the information you put together regarding how everyone's roles are aligned with the goal to tie individual achievement and goals to that larger team goal. This makes sure you are consistent in rewarding the right type of behavior that benefits the group as well as the individual.

Embrace similarities and diversity

A recipe for disaster in any organization is for the team to all have the same skills, background and experiences. In these cases, there are no synergies to be found because there are no unique strengths to focus on, and there aren't any unique weaknesses that can be minimized, 1+1 just equals 2.

The downside of diversity is your team won't all be the same, won't know how to relate to one another, won't understand the strengths and weaknesses of everyone, and won't know how everyone fits into the purpose of the organization. This is a common problem in larger organizations today, and the way to counter it is to get clear on expectations and roles.

Expectations and roles answer all of these questions for your team so they can focus on doing the work:

Expectations: A common set of principles for how everyone will behave and work. This covers not only etiquette, but also specific performance standards.

Roles: What they do and how it fits into the processes and procedures, as well as how it helps the team achieve their goals.

When your team clearly understands what people do, how they do it, and they are all held accountable on an individual and group basis for achieving the goals within this framework, it sets a clear baseline of understanding that eases communication.

ROAD WORK AHEAD

One of the best team building exercises to conduct is to pair employees up and have them try to find as many similarities as possible. Perhaps you have a "theme" like hobbies, work history, food, or just about anything. The team with the most similarities wins. The next time you do it, you switch the teams up. The benefit of this exercise is that in discovering similarities, the team will also uncover differences at the same time. This exercise is a great way for employees to get to know more about each other. And don't forget to include yourself as a participant, your employees are just as interested in finding out about you.

Allies and saboteurs

You aren't starting from scratch in this endeavor. One of the principles of team building is to focus on strengths and to lean on those strengths whenever possible. You already have people on your team who are naturally good at working with others and bringing people together. On the other hand, you have people who are the opposite. So start with what you have:

- Who on your team is already a team building advocate?
- Who on your team is resistant to teamwork?

Identifying who is and isn't already fostering a team environment can be very enlightening. If you look at the areas each of these people work in, you'll likely find areas that are and aren't more team-oriented to correspond with their behavior. So if you're looking for places to start, look to leverage those who are already advocating for teamwork to build consensus. And look to the areas where "resistors" are as areas where some of the biggest and most difficult opportunities lie.

What is working

Team building isn't about just bringing people together; it is a process of addressing specific areas of the operation where you can improve collaboration to improve your progress towards shared goals. You don't just want better teamwork; you want better teamwork that helps you reach goals. One reason initiatives don't get all of the benefits they should be getting out of team building is because they aren't focused, they are general. So let's look at what is working right now:

- What processes have been built in collaboration?
- What tools are you using to foster teamwork?

What doesn't work and why:

- What processes should be collaborating but are struggling to?
- What areas will be naturally difficult to foster teamwork?
- What is missing from both of these to help foster teamwork?
- What barriers exist to teamwork in these areas?

Don't just build your team, build your team to address specific things. One of the ways to manage the process better is to know what areas you are strong and weak in already. Take a look at what is working and what isn't and see if you can start by transferring some lessons from what works to what doesn't.

"If you want to go fast, go alone. **If you want to go far, you need a team."**

~John Wooden

EXPRESSWAY

Team up – One of the easiest ways to increase collaboration and teamwork is to hand out tasks and duties to pairs or teams instead of individuals. While they may split up the task and work on it individually, it is one more way of increasing communication and the times they work together, which will pay off in easier collaboration on other tasks.

Give your team a voice

Much of the discussion to this point has been focused on what you can do, but the power of team building is utilizing not just your own eyes, ears and brain, but the eyes, ears and brains of everybody. For that reason, one of the best places to start when you want to take action, is simply by bringing your team in and asking them:

- "Are there ways we could work better as a team in our own department?"
- "Who do you think you work well with as a team right now?"
- "What areas are you not getting as much help as you think you should?"

This demonstrates the sort of teamwork and collaboration you should expect from your team, and gives you the added bonus of introducing the concept of team building to your team so your initial action steps don't come as a surprise.

A Pothole to Avoid

When you treat everyone on a team the same, without taking into account their strengths and knowledge, you aren't creating teamwork, you're creating robots. Yes, you want an environment of respect and opportunity, but that doesn't mean that you ignore the individual contribution that can be made in specific situations. Leveraging strengths and experience is where diversity creates synergies, and where teamwork gets the results you want. It is a difficult balancing act, which is why many leaders default to treating every individual on the team as an equal in every situation. But if you don't acknowledge and use each person on your team differently based on the situation and their aptitude, you're results will be mediocre, not outstanding.

How to Be Great

Break down silos

The silos that exist both within departments and between departments are caused by priorities and conflicting goals. If you align those two things with collaboration, your silos will break down by themselves.

Silos were created for a good reason; to be able to focus the efforts of teams and management and to be able to monitor productivity at a more granular level. Where they go wrong is when they overlook the benefits to productivity of working across silos. Part of this oversight is the need to break down current processes that work within the silo to address needs outside of the silo. In many cases this would cause a risk of less productivity at the silo level, even though the productivity gains elsewhere would far outweigh it. The leader or employee of that silo would naturally be resistant as they might consider it a backwards step in their performance.

If you want to break down silos you need to address the evaluation process by clearly defining a group vision and goal between departments or entities within the same department. Goals aren't just something to strive for, they are something that affect the decision making process. Where many conflicts arise in organizations is when there are competing or conflicting goals. What is a priority for you and your department is often not a priority for another department because the two of you have different goals? A shared vision and group goals is fundamental to addressing that.

So how do you do it?

The best place to start is actually not with the goal itself, but with the current priorities, conflicts, and effects in the current environment. The reason is that overall organizational goals are typically decided at the very top of the leadership structure and you will need to have some back-up data before addressing this with you and your peer's boss (or bosses).

Start by answering five questions:

- What priorities do you or your department have that are not aligned with another's?
- Put yourself in the place of the other silo—what would make that silo realize your need was a priority?
- What information do you or your department have that could be useful to others?
- What information or assistance do you need from another silo that you are not getting?
- In what areas would increased collaboration and giving up some autonomy be more beneficial for the organization than maintaining your individuality?

If the silos reside under your authority, you can take action on this information and determine ways to address the conflicts through notifications, accommodations and general awareness of the overall goals. If you are working with a cross departmental leader in dealing with the silo, you can either address it the same way you would in your own department, or take the information and recommendations to your bosses.

Friends make everything better

Building friendships is often overlooked when talking about teamwork and collaboration. However, Gallup, in its series *"The twelve key dimensions that describe great workgroups"* found employees are more likely to be willing to collaborate and provide each other with critical feedback when they have developed a close friendship. In fact, employees who report having a friend at work are 27% more likely to report that their opinions seem to count at work.

Encouraging activities that foster friendships by allowing people to find out more about one another, form bonds, and have fun is one of the best ways to build teamwork. Some suggestions:

- Put your employees together in teams to compete towards the monthly goals.
- If they want to put together a Fantasy Football or March Madness contest, let them.
- Have dress up days at work surrounding sports teams, themes, or holidays.
- Do team building activities that focus on uncovering strengths or finding out more about another person.

One of the worst things leaders do is to discourage friendships in the workplace, because they focus only on the negative (cliques, rumors, lower productivity) without considering just how powerful they could be when managed and directed towards the right thing.

EXPRESSWAY

"Google it" – Team building activities have a bad reputation. They aren't all about trust falls and going camping in the woods together. They can be simple 5-10 minute exercises that help the team discover more about each other. Setting a goal of doing one simple team building activity every week, not only makes it more "normal" as opposed to "awkward", it consistently builds better understanding between employees as well as an element of fun. You can simply Google, "Team Building Activities" to find hundreds of simple activities. Pick three to start with, and do one every week for the next three weeks. Once you go through this "trial period" you'll likely be OK with many more of the activities you reviewed before. Plan to keep the momentum going with one every week.

"**How you as the leader model teamwork,** how persistent you are in relying upon it, and how you creatively show its benefits, **will do more than anything else to drive it into your organization.**"

Be a player and a coach

Your example is one of the single most important factors in whether your efforts on team building will be successful. I love the analogy of a leader as a coach, but don't forget your team often looks to you for how to be a great player. When you are collaborating with them and encouraging further collaboration, there is nothing that encourages teamwork more.

Imagine when employees come to you with a question, and instead of answering it, you immediately call over another employee and ask their opinion. What message does that send? That other employees may have insight the original one doesn't? That everyone should be asking the opinions of peers? And that none of us has all of the answers, since even the leader seeks outside advice.

How you as the leader model teamwork, how persistent you are in relying upon it, and how you creatively show its benefits will do more than anything else to drive it into your organization.

ROAD WORK AHEAD

Practice this technique of bringing in outside opinions this week when people are asking your advice. It may seem awkward at the start, but stick with it. You'll soon notice your ability to advertise individual's strengths and experience to their team which will foster better understanding as well as collaboration.

Extend a lifeline

The best aspects of teamwork are when people help other people do what needs to get done. As the leader, creating a "helping" culture is essential in building a great team. So how do you foster it?

You personally assist employees and you ask employees to help others.

Seeing a need and either stepping in to help yourself, or more powerfully, telling someone on the team to come to the aid of their teammate forges the bonds of working together. Of course, you can't let your work or the assisting employee's work suffer, but that can also be a chance for the employee in need to reciprocate the behavior. If you do this at every opportunity you see, you'll forge a "helping culture" that will provide demonstrable examples of how teamwork can help everyone be more productive.

You Know the Route, Now Start Driving

What one tactic from the "Better" or "Great" will you employ now that you are done with the chapter?

What actions will you take to improve?

What date and time will you take action?

When will you review the results?

What is one other tactic you wish to employ when you are satisfied with the results of the first?

Souvenirs From The Trip

How to Be Better
Why are you playing the game?
How to find the right purpose to build a team around.

Embrace similarities and diversity
The two things required to make the most out of diversity.

Allies and saboteurs
An idea of who you can call on to help build the team, and who will take extra persuasion.

What is working
How to leverage what is already in place.

Give your team a voice
Three questions you should ask every employee that will tell you what to work on from a team building standpoint.

A Pothole to Avoid
Why treating everybody the same isn't always what you want to do.

How to Be Great
Break down silos
How to shift the perspective of different departments and areas to show that they really are on one team.

Friends make everything better
How friendship leads to teamwork

Be a player and a coach
Why your personal example is one of the most important aspects of building a team.

Extend a lifeline
One of the most important benefits of teamwork is something you can help along.

"Expressways"
Team up
A simple technique to get your employees working together.

"Google it"
All the team building ideas you could ever ask for.

9

Motivation

Tending the fire so it doesn't
go out

MOTIVATION IS FUEL FOR YOUR EMPLOYEES. IF YOU LET THEM RUN ON EMPTY, THEY WON'T TAKE YOU ANYWHERE.

Are You Heading Down a Dead End?

Do employees immediately notice the negative in every situation?

Is nobody smiling or laughing?

Are employees less cooperative with each other?

Is there a lot of silence in meetings?

Does everything seem to be moving slower?

Getting Fired Up

Motivation is at the heart of leadership. Being able to get your employees to give that little bit "extra" is what separates great leaders from mediocre ones. The ability to bring out the best in your team when you need it most is great, but it only gets at part of the story on motivation and how leaders need to think about it. Good times and bad times come and go in a constant succession, and being able to motivate your team through the bad times can mean the difference between staying there for an extended period of time, or moving right back on to the good times. Motivation isn't something you do just when you have a need, it is something you need to be doing for your employees regularly so they can navigate the ups and downs of work and life in the best way possible.

It's also worth noting that if you go a little deeper into motivation and why it produces our "best efforts" you'll see a whole host of things we've already talked about in this book. When people are motivated, they are more engaged in the organization, they are communicating more, they are more apt to collaborate with others, bring voice to their ideas, point out problems, help others, and generally be the employees we always want them to be. Motivation doesn't get nearly enough credit for being the pathway to a healthy and productive workforce.

When you can build up some energy in your employees and focus it onto specific tasks, it's the recipe for getting great things done.

Why Leaders Take a Wrong Turn

Focused on the operation not people

Leaders are constantly being pulled in two different directions; spending time working with people, and spending time working on the operation. Often, they either take for granted people will be self-motivated, or they just find it easier to work with processes and reports than it is to work with people.

When this happens, employee development and engagement stagnates, and people fall into a "rut" where nothing is changing. When people aren't continually engaged, challenged, or developing, they are far more prone to becoming demotivated.

Focused on fixing things

Leaders tend to be hyper-focused on finding problems that need to get fixed. After all, problems are what gets talked about the most by employees, peers and bosses. It's often what the leader is evaluated on most; how many problems have occurred and what they've done about them. This is how leaders can get caught in the mistaken belief there is more opportunity in fixing the bad things instead of leveraging the good things.

The issue with this is that when a leader's focus is on everything going wrong, nobody is talking about everything going right. This creates a "culture of defeat" where good things are ignored and go unrewarded. Motivation in these environments isn't directed in a positive way, it is used strictly to avoid the negative. That kind of motivation maintains the status quo, and doesn't help organizations and leaders create teams that excel.

"Shouldn't people just do their jobs?"

People are human, and to ignore the emotional aspects of managing employees is to eliminate the greatest purpose and opportunity of leadership. Machines have a defined and finite capacity. When leaders treat their employees like machines, they get a similar finite capacity out of them. This is one of the greater mistakes of leadership, because addressing deeper motivations in employees unlocks more capacity through innovation, teamwork, and feedback.

It may be easier for a leader to ignore motivation, and focus on the argument people just need to complete their job duties, but to do so limits the employees' performance and the overall performance of the organization.

How to Be Better

Show them the "highlight reel"

Positive outcomes motivate people. One of the best things you can do to motivate your team is to simply recognize their successes. The more you talk about success the more motivated your team will be to succeed more. Nobody enjoys working in an environment where their contribution goes unnoticed. Too often leaders are focused on correcting behavior instead of catching them doing something right. Tom Peters said it best, "Celebrate what you want to see more of." When an employee puts forth extra effort to get something done, learns something that will help them in the future, helps a coworker, or exceeds a performance metric, you need to recognize it.

The problem for many leaders is they have so much experience looking for problems, they struggle to pick out the successes all around them. So here are some great places for you to start looking:

- Progress towards individual or group goals
- A great customer interaction
- Learning something new or doing something new for the first time
- Success on key metrics
- Anything relating to better teamwork
- Reaching a milestone

When you start looking for them, you'll start seeing them everywhere. Successes outnumber failures and problems by an incredibly wide margin.

But it isn't just about the individual achievement. Don't forget how much people want to be a part of a winning team. When you are looking for successes, don't neglect the successes of the department and organization as a whole.

A software company I'm familiar with in Silicon Valley that is perennially on the "Best Places to Work" lists sends out a company-wide e-mail every time they bring on a new account. As they've grown, that's turned into two or three e-mails a day.

It's essential you nurture teamwork by calling out the successes of the department and organization as a whole.

ROAD WORK AHEAD

Write out a list of each of your employees and next to their names write down one success each of them has had over the last week. For those who had this success within the last 48 hours, go out and tell them, "Great job on _____." As you become more aware of successes, you should be doing this on close to a daily basis.

"Employees are more **energized and motivated** when they feel that their work has **meaning and importance."**

You don't know what you don't know

Most leaders just guess at what motivates their team, but if you put forth the effort to find out what motivates each member of your team, you'll likely have some eye-opening surprises. And the best way to find out what motivates your team is to simply ask them.

There was a survey, *The 7 Key Trends Impacting Today's Workplace*, conducted by the employee engagement firm TINYpulse, and involved over 200,000 employees in more than 500 organizations. The survey covered a broad range of topics, but there was a specific question the survey asked on motivation: "What motivates you to excel and go the extra mile at your organization?" Employees could choose only one of 10 possible answers. Interestingly, you'll notice that money, which is often assumed to be the biggest motivator, wasn't even in the top five. The actual results are below:

1) (20%) Camaraderie, peer motivation
2) (17%) Intrinsic desire to a good job
3) (13%) Feeling encouraged and recognized
4) (10%) Having a real impact
5) (8%) Growing professionally
6) (8%) Meeting client/customer needs
7) (7%) Money and benefits
8) (4%) Positive supervisor/senior management
9) (4%) Believe in the company/product
10) (9%) Other

When you understand what motivates each of your employees you are able to make informed decisions to shape motivation on not only a team basis, but on an individual basis as well. If you had an unmotivated employee whose motivation modeled the survey above, offering them a monetary incentive and being more positive and upbeat around them would have limited impact (7% and 4% respectively). On the other hand, if your whole team's motivation modeled the above survey and you reorganized the department into collaborative teams, displayed team results publicly for recognition, and ensured everyone knew how important their job was you could impact motivation in the department dramatically by addressing some of the most prevalent drivers (20%, 13%, and 10% of respondents respectively).

ROAD WORK AHEAD

Send an individual e-mail to each member of your team asking them "What motivates you to excel and go the extra mile?" Ask them to select their top three choices from the list of ten above. The reason you want them to give you their top three is people aren't always as self-aware as we would like them to be, so having them pick three helps you create a healthy margin for error that should capture their top motivator and a couple of important ones to them.

It's all about IMPACT

Are you more excited to be working on a project vital to the success of the organization like developing a new product, or something more routine like stocking shelves or filing paperwork? Usually you are more excited by the opportunity to have an impact. However, that is a bit of a trick question, because both areas are critical to the success of the organization, and if you aren't talking about it with your team, you have a huge opportunity in front of you.

Employees are more energized and motivated when they feel their work has meaning and importance. The funny thing is, every aspect of your employees' work *is* critical to the organization's success. If it wasn't, it simply wouldn't be a part of their duties. Think about it. If all of a sudden they weren't there, or a job duty wasn't done, that would be a negative for the organization. Now some people and some duties may be more important and critical than others, but they all have value.

To instill this sense of importance in everything your team does, simply start talking about why tasks are important to what the organization does and how they do it.

- Filing ensures nobody has to waste time looking for things.
- Storage limits on your Inbox are a way to save money on storage so it can be spent on more important things.
- Answering the phone in three rings is the first step in letting the customer know they actually *are* important to us.

To take it to the next level, start doing similar things with their roles and the department itself. Describe how they fit into the operation and how it functions. Once you start looking for and highlighting ways your team is vital to the organization, you'll quickly reinforce your own belief in the value of what you do and oversee.

EXPRESSWAY

The simplest and most powerful motivators are only four words long – "I'm proud of you" and "Good job on that" take only a moment to say, but show recognition and appreciation for an employee's efforts. The effect of this recognition can't be overstated. Nobody wants to work in a place where they aren't appreciated. If you start throwing these two phrases around every day, you'll make work a place your employees enjoy coming to, and you'll make excellence something they want to strive for.

The strong foundation

One of the greatest fears is the fear of the unknown. Unfortunately, too many employees live under this fear every day at work because they don't have clear expectations of what they are supposed to do, what performance standard they are held to, and routinely lack the information necessary to complete projects. How can they be motivated to work if they don't know what to work on, what their goals are, or even how to do it?

Being clear on expectations is a foundational area of motivation that establishes accountability between your employees and you, as well as between employees themselves. The extra few minutes you spend setting expectations and ensuring your employees have all of the information they need is insurance against undermining all of your other efforts in motivating them.

Mirror, mirror, on the wall

Want a more motivated staff? Then be motivated yourself. Your team is always looking to you to see how they should react in certain situations, and they will "mirror" your behavior. When times are tough, wear a smile on your face. When a challenge arises, charge right into it. But what is even more important is to go through your regular day-to-day activities in a way that demonstrates passion, commitment, and joy. When your team sees you acting in this way, they'll be more apt to do the same.

A Pothole to Avoid

The shortcut that many leaders make the mistake of taking with motivation is to motivate out of fear. Threats are something that will get your team moving toward the goal that you set in the short term, but it undermines your leadership in the long term. People operating out of fear aren't working at their best. Fear builds resentment. Fear limits the feedback you get. Fear stifles innovation. Fear may get you what you want in the instant case, but it doesn't show you how much more you could achieve without it. For all of those reasons, leaders who motivate based on fear limit their potential and their team's potential.

How to Be Great

Reach for the stars

Professional development is a huge motivating factor for most of your employees whether they want a promotion, want job security, or just get bored if they aren't learning something new. Your employees want to know you value them enough to invest in their growth. It validates their belief they have potential for greater things, which almost everybody has. By encouraging the employee's development, you are making a personal connection with your employees, drawing out a sense of pride in them and letting them know their learning is as important to you as it is to them.

K.I.S.S. – Keep it simple stupid!

If you want to kill the motivation of your team to do a particular task, all you need to do is make it as difficult as possible to accomplish. On the flip side of that statement, if you want them to be motivated to do something, make it as easy as possible.

A Deloitte Consulting article, *"Simplification of Work: The Coming Revolution"* stated:

"Simplification may be one of the most important and underutilized tools in an organization's arsenal. The opportunity can lie both in simplifying the work environment and in simplifying the work itself.... Companies can "simplify" without being "simplistic"—and the entire organization can benefit as a result."

194

eys to your leadership success is how easy you make it for
) accomplish the goals of the organization. Think back on
boss. Did they strive to make it easy for you to do your
isk yourself the same question about your best boss. This
ely a different answer right? Focus on the following to
i are categorized in the latter category as opposed to the

Create and/or enhance tools to do the job better – Are there tasks you can
work on automating? Is there a new report you can create to give your
people better access to information? Could they use dual monitors?
Sometimes it is as simple as replacing the 4-year-old department
printer with a new one.

Remove unnecessary steps and obstacles – What obstacles does your team
face which prohibit them from completing a task swiftly and
smoothly? Are there approvals that could be replaced with
empowerment? Are there steps in the process not worth the time? Are
there communication challenges that could be addressed with new
procedures? If you don't know the obstacles, then ask your employees
and they will surely mention them to you.

Provide clear direction – Many leaders try to give more details to try to be
clearer, which isn't bad at all, but what you want to do is take a brief
amount of time and explain why you are asking for something to be
done. If you explain why, then the employee can better understand the
direction you have already given and can more easily "fill in the
blanks" in their understanding of direction.

Remove uncertainty – Along with clear direction, make sure you limit the
number of unknowns they may face. The easiest way for you to do
this is to make sure the team knows what the entire plan is. It is
worthwhile to spend the extra minute or more to show where their
effort fits into the lifecycle of the process or task.

Why do these steps improve motivation?

They will get more done – A sense of accomplishment is a reward unto itself. If their tasks are made easier and quicker through the removal of obstacles and the enhancement of tools and processes to accomplish more then they will feel better about the work they do and be motivated to do it, not dread doing it.

Less oversight – When you are clear in your direction, have explained to your team why a course of action is needed, and have explained the plan from start to finish there is less need for you to stand over their shoulders and monitor progress. This empowers your team to do things themselves which leads to ownership. Less micromanagement, more control over how they work, and more ownership over the result are all things that help motivation.

Fewer errors – Nobody likes making mistakes. Since simple and easy tasks leave less room for error than difficult and complicated tasks, your team will be less likely to feel concern over making a mistake. Couple that with being clearer about anticipated outcomes and you have a win-win.

And don't forget that keeping things simple has a ton of benefits for the productivity of the organization as well; speed, less training time, easier innovation, and more.

"People often say that motivation doesn't last. **Well, neither does bathing,** that's why we recommend it daily."

~Zig Ziglar

EXPRESSWAY

Special events – If you worry that the day-to-day routine of your employees' jobs may get them down, then try celebrating some special events from time to time. This can be dress up days for holidays, celebrating birthdays and anniversaries, pot-lucks, or holding any random event. People enjoy having fun at work and breaking things up. This sort of thing may not seem like motivation, but putting a smile on people's faces is exactly that.

The power of purpose

If your motivation plan for your team requires constant games and contests, or your constant involvement, you are destined to fail, or at least get only marginal results. To get the foundational motivation you are looking for you need something that gives meaning to even the simplest of tasks. You need to answer the question, "Why is what we all do here important?" This makes the long hours of routine work bearable, brings meaning to training, and breeds a sense of teamwork around a common vision.

These are typically known as Mission Statements or Core Values in most organizations. Now don't worry, they are actually relatively simple to put together in a two-step process, and if you create the right "reason" for your team, motivation can become self-sustaining.

1st Step: Why are you there – You need to define the reason and purpose for the existence of your department or organization. For some it may be, "bring in new customers", "create a great experience", "perfection in processing", "create innovative products", "lightning fast resolution" or many others. What is your fundamental purpose in the organization?

2nd Step: Make it special – You want to add some "oomph" to the mission. What would happen if your department didn't exist? What do you do particularly well or extraordinarily that your competitors don't? How does what you do help other departments or the customer? This step highlights why you are important. People want to do things that matter, and this step focuses on that.

Some examples of what you could come up with for particular departments:

- I.T. – "We handle the digital needs of the company so everyone can work at peak performance"
- Retail Sales Agents – "We match the customer's desires to the perfect product so they can go confidently through their day"
- Sales – "We bring in new clients so the organization can grow and thrive"
- Customer Support – "We take care of the customer's needs and wants so they can get the most out of our products and services"
- Accounting – "We keep track of the financial lifeblood of the organization so it can run in an efficient and informed manner"

Once you have a Mission Statement, what do you do? Well, suffice to say that an effective purpose is put into practice by tying it to as many practical applications as possible. It's talked about and used to make decisions and do great work, not put up on a poster that everyone ignores. If you as the leader speak about the purpose constantly, and publicly drive the Mission Statement home, then your team can start making the correlation between everything they do and a purpose that is inspiring and energizing.

And that is the whole point of a purpose; to inspire and motivate your team in everything they do.

Arts and crafts time

Discovering something new is always exciting. Exercising creativity is something that breaks up monotony and gets our minds thinking about possibilities and opportunities. Even for those of us who aren't the most innovative or creative thinkers, tapping into creativity is an inherently positive pastime. Brainstorming activities about problems or opportunities, letting someone run with their idea for something, working alongside different people, or even just decorating the department can bring a positive break to an otherwise routine day and unleash good ideas.

ROAD WORK AHEAD

Create a "Fun Committee" for your organization. This group of volunteers will be tasked with decorating the workplace for holidays, coordinating birthday celebrations, and coordinating at least one "fun" activity a quarter. Encourage everyone to be a part of it and let them take over these areas so you don't have to. This gives members of your team a chance to exercise that creativity, and instills a sense of ownership.

This can also be an opportunity for someone to step up into leadership if you create "Fun Committee Chair" or 'Fun Committee Lead" positions.

Cull your worst performers

One of the hardest things to do is to make the right decision for the organization and your employees and let people go who continue to have disciplinary or performance issues that haven't been resolved after multiple warnings. Obviously you need to have done everything in your power as their leader to correct and train the behavior you want to see, but it will become a reality at some point in your career. There are two things that occur when you do this:

It's a form of recognition – Your superior performers want to know everybody is being held to the same standards they regularly hold themselves to. While you should be recognizing their performance regularly, if people who aren't performing are held accountable, that is a recognition itself.

You gain the respect of the team – Letting someone go is the most difficult action a leader can take, and your employees know it. This is one of the most powerful ways you can lead by example and show your commitment to excellence. When the leader is willing to make the tough choice for the good of the organization, your team will be more likely to as well.

Nobody likes to see someone fail, but it is also demotivating to see a double-standard in performance. Poor performers, or those with disciplinary issues, are a weight that everyone on the team carries. Letting go of that weight can lift the performance, and also the spirits, of those on the team.

You Know the Route, Now Start Driving

What one tactic from the "Better" or "Great" will you employ now that you are done with the chapter?

What actions will you take to improve?

What date and time will you take action?

When will you review the results?

What is one other tactic you wish to employ when you are satisfied with the results of the first?

Souvenirs From The Trip

How to Be Better
Show them the "highlight reel"
Why you might be talking about the wrong thing, and how to get yourself back on track.

You don't know what you don't know
Why leaders might be surprised what really motivates their team.

It's all about IMPACT
How to use people's sense of importance to guide you in motivating them.

The strong foundation
This basic job principle sets the tone for all of your efforts on motivation.

Mirror, mirror, on the wall
Why your reactions can determine how motivated your staff is.

A Pothole to Avoid
Why fear is the worst motivation shortcut you could ever take.

How to Be Great
Reach for the stars
How your team's desire for development has a secondary benefit regarding morale.

K.I.S.S. – Keep it simple stupid!
Three reasons simplicity matters when trying to motivate your staff.

The power of purpose
How to develop a Mission Statement that will motivate your team through every task they conduct.

Arts and crafts time
Why developing a creative outlet for people improves morale.

Cull your worst performers
Two reasons terminating your poor performers drives positive morale.

"Expressways"
The simplest and most powerful motivators are only four words long
Two phrases that will make your team enjoy working for you.

Special events
The power of a party.

1 Listening
Without information you can't lead effectively

2 Prioritizing
Ensure your work isn't a waste

3 Delegation
The greatest struggle and opportunity in leadership

4 Communication
The prerequisite for success

5 Micromanagement
When control is counter productive

6 Dealing with Failure
Your inevitable opportunity

7 Hiring
The most lasting decision

8 Team Building
Making 1+1=3

9 Motivation
Tending the fire so it doesn't go out

10 Developing Yourself
Your growth helps everyone

10.

Developing Yourself

Your growth helps everyone

DON'T BE SO BUSY LEADING OTHERS THAT YOU FORGET TO LEAD YOURSELF

Are You Heading Down a Dead End?

Has it been a while since you've been challenged?

Do you struggle to think of something you learned recently?

Would you describe yourself as "comfortable" in your work?

Has it been a while since someone praised your work?

What are your career goals? Do you have any clear ones?

Do you figure that development happens naturally as you gain experience?

Chapter Intro

One of the most overlooked ways to improve the performance of your team is your own self-development. It may seem counter-intuitive, but a leader is rarely more impactful than when they are learning themselves. It sets an example for initiative, personal development, and achievement for your team to follow. As a leader, your personal skills and abilities will either be magnified and leveraged for the benefit of your whole team, or your lack of abilities and skills will weigh down your employees' performance. In this way, it could be argued nobody's development in the organization is more important than the leader's.

In this discussion it is also important to never forget that you owe it to yourself as well. You have a responsibility to your employees, you have a responsibility to your organization, and you have a responsibility to yourself. Where burnout and career stagnation come into play most often is when those three "stakeholders" for your time get out of balance. The challenge of learning something new is invigorating. The sense of accomplishment once you master something is exhilarating. It is these things that provide motivation for getting through the day-to-day tasks and are rocket fuel for your career.

Every great leader has been a great learner. So if you are committed to being great in your own career, then your own development, learning, and growth needs to be a priority.

Why Leaders Take a Wrong Turn

Too focused on managing others

The #1 reason most leaders aren't developing themselves as much as they should be is they are too focused on operational results and developing others. This is a classic, "too much of a good thing" scenario, where their heart is in the right place, but their actions are undermining their best efforts.

You will never hear me say to not invest in the development of your employees. That is the heart of leadership. But when leaders put themselves last and neglect their development for too long, that stagnation can have an effect on not only on their career, but on all of those around them.

You're comfortable where you are

A lot of the time leaders resist development and growth because they (rightly) associate it with work. Many leaders reach a short-term or medium term goal in their career and start weighing the benefits of continuing up the career ladder with the costs associated with that climb. If they are going to move up the ladder, it's going to take effort that may or may not be worth it to them.

That is all well and good, but where the mistake in that thinking lies is in thinking too short-term. Development in our ever-changing world isn't just about growing. Development is required just to maintain our effectiveness in a world that is moving forward. As the old saying goes, "If you're not growing, you're dying."

Yes, development often leads to promotion, but that is often a by-product of simply doing a great job. If you want to keep doing a great job you need to keep developing yourself.

Consider it a given

Experience is useless if you don't spend time evaluating it and acting on what you learn from that evaluation. Too many leaders, and people in general, just figure that as they gain weeks, months, and years of experience they will just naturally grow. That simply isn't the case.

Leaders see that all of the time in front-line employees who have been in the same position for years and years. Are they guaranteed to be better the more time they spend in the position? Absolutely not. In many cases they actually regress. There's a lesson for every leader in that example.

Nobody does it for them

"But my company doesn't have a leadership development program." This is the excuse you might hear from a leader who isn't prioritizing their own development. Obviously it would be great if somebody else set up the structure and held us accountable for our learning, but if that isn't the case, it doesn't give the leader a free-pass. There are innumerable resources that can help with leadership development; books, online courses, and mentors to name a few. If you want something, you need to be willing to go out and get it yourself.

How to Be Better

Lost in Wonderland

When you think about it, creating a personal development goal and plan is the most important, yet most overlooked, thing you can do for your career. Yes, so many leaders manage their careers in a way that reminds me of the following scene from Alice in Wonderland, by Lewis Carroll;

"Would you tell me, please, which way I ought to go from here?"

"That depends a good deal on where you want to get to," said the Cat.

"I don't much care where—" said Alice.

"Then it doesn't matter which way you go," said the Cat.

"—so long as I get SOMEWHERE," Alice added as an explanation.

"Oh, you're sure to do that," said the Cat, *"if you only walk long enough."*

Oh, they want to get promoted, they want to get more responsibility, they want more money, but they aren't specific as to what it really is. They are still likely to get progress, but they may not end up where they hoped to because they weren't clear on their intent. The clearer you can be on exactly where you want your career to end up, the better the chances of you making it there, the quicker you will get there, and the easier it is to come up with a specific plan. So let's get you started:

- What is the next position you want to be promoted into? Supervisor, Shift Manager, Sales Manager, etc.
- What is the long term position you are shooting for? Store Manager, Division Manager, Operations Manager, Chief Operating Officer, etc.
- What weaknesses should you address? Delegating, Listening, Motivation, Process Design, etc.

- What strengths should you continue to develop? Analysis, Communication, Team Building, etc.

- What traits do successful people have in the position you're looking at? What do they do, what are they good at, how do they lead? Are they adept at any particular programs or processes? Do they exhibit any particular traits like Patience, Flexibility, or Thoughtfulness?

- What traits and skills should you cultivate? Excel, Patience, Understanding a P&L, Market Dynamics, etc.

- What trade publications are available? If you're looking to move into the Executive ranks, or even if you just want to understand the industry better, you'll need to be able to speak the language. Almost every single industry on Earth has some sort of trade publication or magazine, and usually they make content available online.

- What resources are out there that can help you? Online courses, "Excel for Dummies" books, magazines, self-help books, you're looking for a way to jump start the process as best you can and give you some structure to your development.

When you are crystal clear on your goal, what it looks like to reach that goal, and the resources you have available to you, then putting together the steps of a plan gets much easier.

Put a GPS on your goals

The plan is great, but remember that a goal loses its power when you don't put deadlines behind it, and here is where tracking progress comes in. Whatever plan you create, you need to put some deadlines and milestones to it. This doesn't mean you say, "I want to be Vice-President in three years." It means you acquire the skills and traits necessary to be a Vice-President and you put deadlines behind the acquiring of each of those. When you put together milestones and a timeline you can manage your expectations and priorities better, and that's where you build the structure behind your plan and focus yourself on the actions to attain it.

One of the important things to find are metrics to track progress. This gives you a "black and white" assessment of how you are doing and fosters better accountability. Think of weight loss or athletic programs as a model of clear and steady progress. For you it may be sales increase percentages, cost saving percentages, output or production numbers. Or in the case of learning, it can simply be covering a chapter a week in a book. The more you come up with metrics, the clearer your progress will be and the more assured you can be of reaching your goal.

ROAD WORK AHEAD

Schedule a meeting with yourself once a month to review your goals and your progress towards those goals. This review should also include whether your goals have changed and whether your plan needs to be adjusted based on that, or the progress you are making. Just once a month for 15-30 minutes can keep you on track and will likely speed your progress up the career ladder.

Managing up

Great leaders are also great followers. Their ability to work with and manage their boss allows them to gain more experience and accomplish more than if they didn't work on that relationship. But beyond the personal gain, it is also beneficial to the organization and your boss if you are supporting them and helping them be as effective as possible.

Your boss holds the key to some of the most important aspects of your development, and learning how to get them to use that key for your benefit can be one of the most important things you do. But make no mistake; managing your boss isn't manipulating your boss, and it also isn't one sided at all. It's about working together as a team to accomplish both of your goals. To do this you need to work on a few things:

First you have to understand them

It's hard to manage anything if you don't understand it, and this goes especially for people. You first want to get clear on what your boss's goals are: What are they working towards? What targets do they need to hit? What is their boss looking for from them? Second, you want to ensure you know what their expectations are for you and your team? Some of these may fall in line with their goals, but many of them are pet peeves and ways of doing business that if you understand, you can keep from getting tripped up by. Thirdly, you need to understand their communication style, otherwise it will be difficult to get your point across. Do they prefer e-mail, text, phone, or in person communication? Do they hate any of those? Do they always want the details, or just the overview? When is the best time to talk to them, the morning, afternoon, lunch?

Getting an understanding of where your boss is coming from helps you align your priorities and communication so you are both on the same page.

You usually have to give before you receive

Reciprocity is one of the principles of negotiation. Give first, then you are free to ask in return. Before you are in a position to ask for more responsibility, ask for more empowerment, or ask to do things your way, you need to establish that you are trustworthy in all of those areas by demonstrating it.

Be exceptional – There is no managing around being great at your job. This is the "price of admission" to gaining trust with your boss. If they can't trust you to handle your current responsibilities well, then there really isn't anything more to discuss.

Be predictable – Trust is all about knowing what is going to happen. Whether it is predictability about the quality of your work, showing up on time to meetings, or how you deal with customer interactions. The more predictable your performance, the more trust you will build.

Keep them informed – Feeding your boss timely and actionable information is one of the most important responsibilities of an employee. This doesn't mean gossiping, this means making them aware of opportunities, potential problems, and simple status updates on what is going on. Keep them informed and they'll be more likely to keep you informed.

Have a great attitude – Nobody wants to be around the person who can find the problem in every situation. Bosses want solutions, not more problems (they have plenty). People are naturally attracted to those who smile and have a positive, "can-do" spirit. If you project that, they'll be more open to your presence.

When you give in each of these areas, you make it easy for your boss to develop trust in you, and you have a foundation with which to begin asking and receiving.

Make their job easier

Do you have an overflowing plate of things to do? Of course you do, and it's a safe bet to think your boss does as well. One of the best ways to be both be a resource to your boss and grow your experience, is to find ways to make their job easier.

Ask to help – Do you want them to help you with something? Then you better have already asked them if there was something you could help with. You want to be a resource for your boss, just like you want them to be a resource for you. Is there a report you can work on for them? Is there a presentation you can help them put together? Is there a meeting you can go to in their place to free up their time? Regularly ask if there's anything you can take off their plate, and eventually they'll take you up on it.

Anticipate – Arnold Glasow once said, "One of the tests of leadership is the ability to recognize a problem before it becomes an emergency." The easiest way to fix a problem is before it happens. Get used to anticipating where your team and your own resources could be best spent and you'll see the operation run much smoother. This makes your job easier and your boss' job easier.

Cover for weaknesses – Every person has weaknesses. Maybe your boss doesn't communicate with your team well, so you can step in and fill in the blanks. Maybe they are terrible at Excel, and you can take that off their hands. Maybe they get frustrated or angry easily and you can find ways to mend the wounds left in their wake, or calm them down in the first place.

Once you have covered all of those areas, you've established a relationship with your boss that allows both of you to maximize the other to accomplish the goals you have set as a team, as well as individual goals as well.

EXPRESSWAY

Every day is a training day – One of the most powerful concepts to put into practice in your career is to consider every day a day where you intend to learn something. This is most often associated with the military and sports, but it absolutely applies to leadership. It could be anything; it could be a process, an insight into how an employee thinks, or another department. Leading with a mindset of curiosity and learning it is like compounding interest for your career.

"You get the best out of others when you get the best out of yourself."

~Harvey S. Firestone

Bloom where you're planted

There is this myth of the "perfect" job that tricks leaders into thinking less of the position and responsibilities they currently have. I don't believe there are any "perfect" jobs out there, but I do think there are a whole lot of "great" jobs out there. The way you get great jobs is by performing exceptionally in *every* job you have. The responsibilities you have now, and how you execute them in the environment you are in, are your audition for better things. If you do great in your audition, then you get the position.

Every workplace and every position has it's struggles. Don't focus only on the things you wish would change, look at the opportunities you have and focus on doing your best with those. That will get you further than anything else.

A Pothole to Avoid

Developing yourself is a marathon, not a sprint. One of the ways leaders derail their own development is in getting greedy for results. You are likely to get some quick wins and make some big strides forward when you first start, and that's great. It validates that you're on the right track. Beyond that, you may find yourself in a period where you are making steady progress. Eventually though, you'll hit a plateau, and your forward progress will seem to stop. The mistake leaders make is they want to continue getting better at the same rate. But this isn't how self-improvement works. The better you get at something, the more effort it will take to reach that "next level." But true leaders learn to love this process; they accept their plateaus as part of learning.

How to Be Great

Sending out an S.O.S.

One of the most uncomfortable things for a leader to do is to admit they don't know the answer, or can't do it all themselves. You can't be the expert at everything, and you can't do everything yourself. Therefore, the best way to guard against mediocre or substandard work is to use the help of the right people on your team. Remember, your job as a leader is to bring out the best effort of those on the team to accomplish the organizational goals. That means putting people in a position to work more in areas of strength than weakness. Why wouldn't you treat yourself the same way.

Asking for help also opens you and your coworkers up to a number of other benefits

- Empowerment
- Skill development
- Better rapport with peers
- A sense of value
- Approachability
- And many more…

If you want to develop faster, use the people with the resources and skills that you have around you to learn from and bring into projects to do just that.

ROAD WORK AHEAD

There is something on your To-Do list right now that you need help with, and honestly, there are probably several. Either you need someone with a skill, you need to delegate it, or you just need more effort than one person can give.

Find out who has the skill or resource and ask them this instant if they could help you. Go ahead, put down the book and do it. Great leaders are humble enough to ask for help, so be great!

Turning your career into a haunted house

We hit on this concept in the section on dealing with failure, but we are going to add to it here. Growth and development happens when you push yourself past what you have already known. Part of the reason people stagnate in their development is a fear of the unknown surrounding the next "test" that pushes that development.

If you want to develop faster, then get scared at every opportunity you can. Volunteer to present at the next Executive meeting, have that overdue and uncomfortable conversation about poor performance with an employee, put yourself in front of a customer and try to do your employee's job to understand how it feels, take a calculated risk and try something new, admit you don't know something, whatever it is you should do or need to do. If you're a little fearful, that's good. It's similar to a test in high school; you'll get through to the other side and be better prepared for the next one.

The simple practice of overcoming your fears can liberate your thinking about possibility, and speed not only your development, but your workflow as well. How many times were you procrastinating on something you didn't want to do because you were afraid of the outcome? Get comfortable being scared, it's how you develop.

"You can't be the expert at everything, **and you can't do everything yourself.** Therefore, the best way to guard against mediocre or substandard work **is to use the help of the right people on your team."**

Chaos can be opportunity

When a crisis hits is often when you learn the most about yourself and those around you. It's when the spotlight shines brightest on you for others to see your worth, and it's where you find a true test of your leadership abilities. Embracing chaos and crisis when they occur helps you perform better in the middle of it, but also stretches your abilities into new areas (out of necessity) and will help you continue your growth. Of course, you don't want these situations to occur, but don't lose sight of this small silver lining, remember "this is what they pay me for," and jump headlong into it. Your most uncomfortable moments in your career are often your greatest opportunities to develop.

ROAD WORK AHEAD

Experience doesn't matter if you don't evaluate the experience to extract the learning. Your last crisis is a great place to start learning. What did you learn about yourself? Were you calm? Did you involve others in the solution? What could you have done better? Where did you excel? The answers to these questions will identify strengths and weaknesses you can work with and develop.

And since leadership isn't just about you, ask the same questions of employees and peers who were involved. This helps you better manage and lead everyone on the team.

Fast track your development

The thing that can speed up your development more than anything else is to find a way to leverage the experience of those who are further along the path you are on. The greatest "hack" for almost any endeavor is experience. In the organizational environment, that means finding a mentor. Ideally that may be your boss, but there are plenty of ways to get the benefits of mentoring outside of the more traditional route and we'll go through them all:

Traditional Mentors – Whether it is help with specific traits and skills, or whether it is help with your career; finding and working with a mentor can be one of the most impactful things in your career. The simple reason is they have been in your shoes before and can show you the path they took without the pitfalls they experienced. They also have a different perspective and viewpoint on matters within the organization which can be enormously enlightening. In the case of specific traits and skills, they know best how to teach others since they've done it before.

"Build a mentor" – You may be in a situation where a mentor is not available to you, but that doesn't need to hold you back. While there may not be someone in your organization who possesses all of the traits of a great leader, there are likely people within your organization who are fantastic in particular areas of leadership you can turn to for specific areas of advice. I personally used this technique throughout my career where I could turn to someone for operational questions, another for sales questions, and yet another for employee relations questions.

Look to what successful people are doing – Similar to the "build a mentor" philosophy is simply looking at how others have achieved success or are achieving success. Simply looking and learning is a great habit to get into (and a central part of making "Every Day a Training Day" work for you). Even if you don't have the ability to engage with others, you can observe them. In this way you can make CEOs of other companies a part of your experience building team. Professional sports athletes, leaders in other verticals, and a host of others have plenty they can teach you if you're looking.

We may learn best from our own mistakes, but it is a whole lot easier to learn from the mistakes and experiences of others. If you aren't looking to be mentored, you're missing out.

EXPRESSWAY

No shortcuts – If you want to be better than others, if you want to advance faster in your career, then you need to be willing to do what others won't. Even if you are lucky enough to have a mentor or an organization that has a leadership development program, when it comes to your personal development, you have to be willing to "go the extra mile." The reason is you will be pulled by competing priorities over your entire career, so if you want to have time for your own growth, you're going to need to make the time to work on that growth. Too many leaders go the "extra mile" on their job, but never do so with themselves. Be sure you're balancing how much "extra mile" effort you put in with the job and yourself to make sure neither is neglected.

Get engaged

Your most important relationship for your career development is the one you have with your boss. The more time spent communicating with them and being exposed to them, the better. They are likely in the position you would naturally grow into, so by spending time with them you are basically researching what their struggles are, what traits help them, what traits hurt them, and generally how they see their role and the role of others. They have access to information that will help give you better perspective on doing your job and helping others.

They also have the most vested interest in your success. Even in cases where you may not be their "favorite," they want you to succeed so they can. They hold the key to what priorities you need to address in your work. They are the one who assigns responsibilities. And they are the one who evaluates the work. So regardless of whether they are your mentor or not, they need to be a part of your list of people to gather experience from.

You Know the Route, Now Start Driving

What one tactic from the "Better" or "Great" will you employ now that you are done with the chapter?

What actions will you take to improve?

What date and time will you take action?

When will you review the results?

What is one other tactic you wish to employ when you are satisfied with the results of the first?

Souvenirs From The Trip

How to Be Better
Lost in Wonderland
Questions you need to answer to give yourself the best chance of developing into the leader you want to be.

Put a GPS on your goals
How to know you're developing.

Managing up
How to make the most out of your boss, for your own development and the good of the organization.

Bloom where you're planted
Why the "grass is always greener" line of thinking is destroying your career growth.

A Pothole to Avoid
Why some leaders stop developing even after making progress.

How to Be Great
Sending out an S.O.S.
One of the most powerful examples a leader can make of themselves.

Turning your career into a haunted house
Why you should be happy about being scared from time to time.

Chaos can be opportunity
The opportunity for you and others to discover what you're made of.

Fast track your development
Three ways others can lead the way for your career growth.

Get engaged
Why your relationship with your boss should be a top priority.

"Expressways"
Every day is a training day
A simple concept that dramatically speeds up your understanding and development.

No shortcuts
How to separate yourself from the competition.

LET'S CONTINUE THE CONVERSATION

Now that you've reached the end of "The Roadmap," you might be wondering what the next step is. Well since I have your attention and this is my book, let me suggest a couple of next steps to keep your leadership progressing and our relationship intact:

Facebook
www.facebook.com/CameronLMorrissey

I conduct LIVE Q&A sessions twice a week, post instructional videos on leadership, and post a number of other thoughts and inspirations. If you haven't checked out my page before, it's well worth the time.

The Leadership Playbook
www.cameronmorrissey.com/leadershipplaybook
Coupon: ROADMAP50

For those interested in really taking their leadership to the next level, The Leadership Playbook is my daily email coaching sessions. You and I address one topic for just 3-5 minutes a day. This gets you steady leadership development in a simple and flexible format. It really is the best thing that I've ever put together for leaders. Check out the webpage, you can sign up for a free one-week trial, and see if it's right for you. As a bonus, use the coupon code above to get 50% off your first month.

E-mail
cm@cameronmorrissey.com

You can always reach out to me directly with any questions you have, or to just say "Hi!" I always answer my own e-mails and it would be great to hear from you.

ABOUT THE AUTHOR

The Official Version – *Cue the movie trailer voice:* One of the most popular thought leaders in management and leadership. Cameron is a real world manager offering advice from his 20+ years of management experience to over 1,000,000 subscribers to his blog and social media channels. His background encompasses Fortune 500 Companies, small companies and government agencies. Cameron writes to help front-line managers and supervisors excel and build teams that drive results. Cameron currently resides in Las Vegas, NV with his wife and three children.

My version – *No deep voice needed:* I'm a manager and have been for a while. I've dealt with all of the common situations like office politics, not finding anyone to hire, unreasonable customers, employees not reaching their potential, holiday in retail, and hundreds of others. So I think one of the reasons my blog and social media have been so popular is I try not to put anything out there I don't believe will work in the real world. Straight talk, practical and actionable advice, that's what I strive for. Hope the movie trailer voice guy isn't mad I left my version in.

My Purpose – If you don't have goals you don't have direction. The best goals are simple and there aren't too many of them. To that end, here are my two career goals:

Goal #1 - To have a positive effect on 8,000,000 leaders around the globe through speaking engagements, coaching clients, and book sales (Facebook doesn't count unfortunately). There is a reason for that number, but to find out the reason you'll have to e-mail me at cm@cameronmorrissey.com, and I'll explain why that's my "dent in the universe," as Steve Jobs said.

Goal #2 – Teach a class at my alma mater, The University of Washington Foster School of Business. I like to think that I'd teach one heck of a fun and practical class.

45239462R00152

Made in the USA
San Bernardino, CA
03 February 2017